INTO THE EARTH

A WINE CAVE RENAISSANCE

DANIEL D'AGOSTINI WITH MOLLY CHAPPELLET

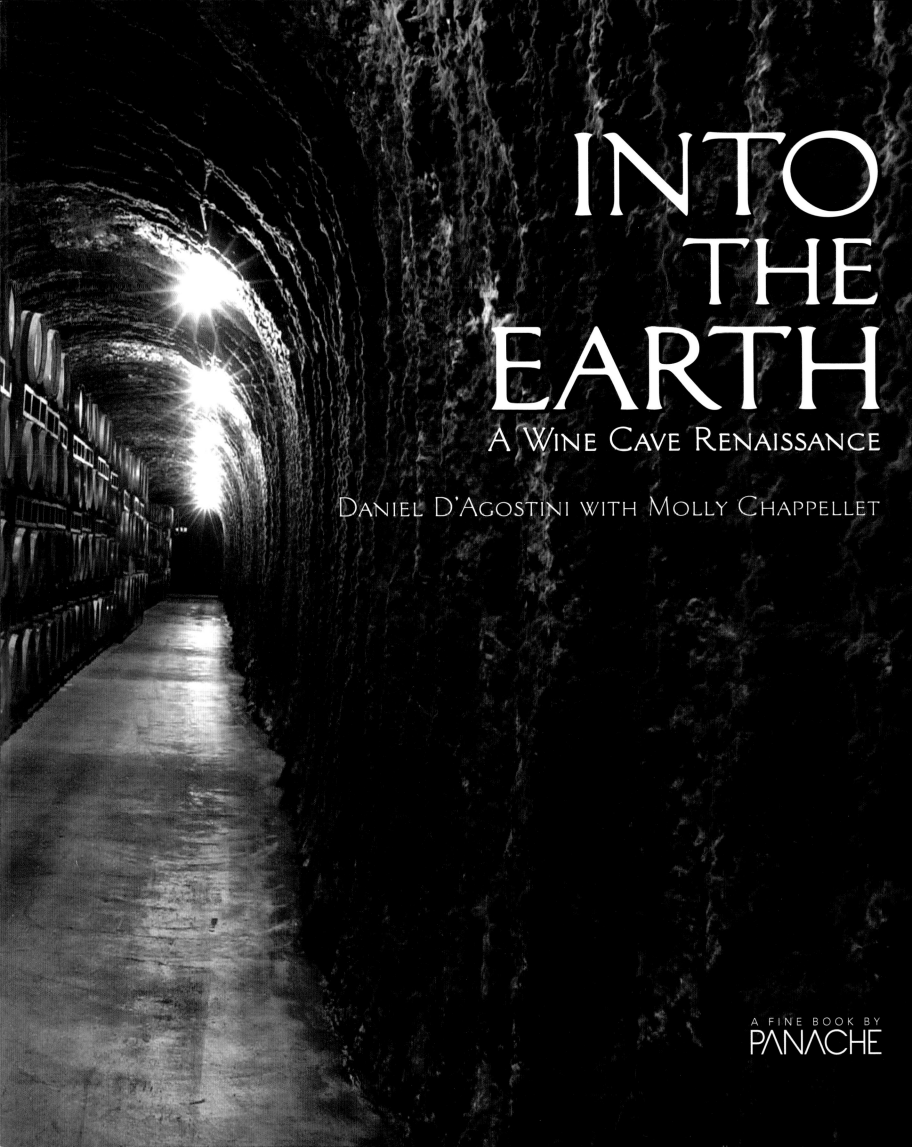

INTO
THE
EARTH
A Wine Cave Renaissance

Daniel D'Agostini with Molly Chappellet

A FINE BOOK BY
PANACHE

To Alf Burtleson, Dale Wondergem, Glen Ragsdale and Graham Wozencroft
as well as the late Gil Nickel who first said, "Let's build a cave."

Foreword

"Wine cellar" trips off the tongue so naturally that you might think wine's natural home is underground. It is certainly its ideal home, quiet, dark and cool—but very little of the world's wine has the privilege of such perfect storage. In the old wine world of Europe, Bordeaux, where standards are set for the world, has few cellars. In Burgundy, most are small and domestic. Only Champagne has caves, vast caverns and labyrinthine tunnels—and that only by the happy chance that Romans quarried them for stone 2,000 years ago.

What other caves have been co-opted for aging wine? There are troglodyte caverns along the Loire, more Roman quarries in Trier on the Mosel and cliff-perched cellars with alarming sea views on Santorini in the Aegean, but you have to go to California to see the idea carried into perfection with all the energy and skill of modern engineering.

It started in the 19th century with Chinese labor. I have particularly fond memories of the coolie-cut Schramsberg caves where Molly Chappellet once planned the surprise party of a lifetime for my birthday. Imagine being deep in the earth with a flickering lantern, when suddenly lights come on to reveal a flowering garden. That is what Molly created: a rare trellis, a little lawn, and my desk with its photos and papers transported to the bowels of the earth. There is clearly something about caves that spurs creativity—and that marriage of talent, wine and holes in the rock has taken off in Napa Valley as nowhere else on earth.

The Channel Tunnel from England to France was dug in the 1980s. When it was finished they parked one of the two immense boring machines by the Dover Road with a sign: For Sale, One Careful Owner. Little did I think it would duly arrive in California with a mission to continue what the coolies started and create the most extensive and spectacular caves ever purpose-made for perfecting wine.

Perhaps this remarkable book only represents the beginning. Perhaps with the constraints of climate change and building restrictions we are going to see other industries, or parts of them, transferred to subterranean seclusion. If this is so, cave-cutting has had an astonishingly creative start.

Hugh Johnson

Preface

In 1996 Daphne Araujo opened the door to her wine cave, and I stepped into a beautiful room full of soft warm light accenting gracefully arched walls. A row of 60-gallon French oak barrels receded down the center. It was inviting and captivating.

When I photographed that enchanting space at Araujo Estate there were less than 40 of these "modern caves," and few people had ever heard about them. By 1998 the paradigm was shifting, and within a decade more than 100 new wine caves were created.

Building underground has not only contributed to the process of making fine wine, it also merits top marks economically and environmentally. Agricultural land does not have to be used to build warehouse facilities with high energy requirements. Some of the greenest projects happening today are led by wineries utilizing wine caves as part of their winemaking process. There are now many examples of valuable vineyards growing directly above the tunnels storing their wine.

With my cameras I began a path of exploration and discovery using film in various formats ranging from 35mm to 4x5. In 2001 a switch to digital gave me greater abilities and productivity in photographing these dark, wondrous spaces.

During the 1860s, about the time that wine caves were first hand-dug in Napa Valley hillsides, Charles Waldeck and Timothy O'Sullivan became the first photographers to record images made in a cave or tunnel. Waldeck made the world's first cave photograph in Mammoth Cave, Kentucky, in 1866 and the following year O'Sullivan was the first to photograph the interior of a mine. O'Sullivan took a great risk when he carried his bulky equipment several hundred feet down into the Comstock Mine in Virginia City, Nevada, and used a pile of magnesium as a flash source to clearly illuminate a miner working with a pickax.

Photographing excavated tunnels and caves in the 21st century is a lot easier than O'Sullivan had experienced. Today I travel light with a sturdy tripod and a camera that beautifully records existing light in these settings without added flash.

Though all wine caves share a common function and are similar in many ways, each is unique. The wine caves portrayed in this book are bored tunnels that range from purely utilitarian to amazingly elaborate. Photographing in a finished cave can be sheer visual pleasure with cool air scented by wine and oak and sometimes tinged with curing cement. Stillness, followed by echoes of the shutter, captures the scene.

During construction, photographing is much more demanding yet presents unique opportunity. It's boots-and-hardhat work—wetness, dust, noise, moving equipment and spraying shotcrete are constant hazards. There have been a few special moments when I have been privileged to witness rare and beautiful geological formations—works of art in themselves—slices of the earth visible only until shotcrete is applied and the drilling continues.

Over the course of many visits an understanding of the creation process becomes clear. Successive trips to photograph Quintessa's cave during the mining phase, for example, clarified my understanding that a tunnel is created from the top down. Photographing a roadheader at work required walking in a level tunnel for about 100 feet to a place where the tunnel's exposed earth floor inclined steeply. There the roadheader could be seen further up, clawing away. I hiked up and set my tripod with one leg fully extended and the other two short as I was squished under curving arches of reinforcing steel on a steep incline of loose earth in close proximity to a 30-ton, 25-foot machine grinding away the exposed rock. About a month later I went back to continue my documentary and first looked around to find the spot where I had been scrunched up with a tripod and camera alongside that enormous machine. I finally located the place, about 16 feet in the air, under the domed ceiling of a cavernous room.

In this journey of photographing wine caves I gained more than photographic insight. I discovered a core of pioneers—visionaries, really—that led this renaissance, along with a huge supporting cast of workers, professionals and artisans. I met people whose passionate stewardship of the earth not only led them into it but shines in their stellar agricultural practices upon it. I even discovered cave doors made from staves of barrels once full of my family's wine.

A clear chronology of this wine-cave phenomenon could not be found in any one place. A book to hold this story was needed. Of course with new caves continually being created the story will still unfold. These words and images provide a portal for learning about what has transpired from the first modern wine caves to those created by midwinter 2009.

Daniel D'Agostini

Introduction

1980s

1990s

2000s

Underground Perspectives

The Myth, Mystery and Magic of Caves

What happens within the earth, in caves hidden from sound, light and movement? Caves evoke a sense of awe and wonder, calling for exploration. Whether formed of rock at the seaside or tunneled in a mountainside at the edge of the desert, caves bid us to enter. We respond. Perhaps we have discovered a secret—a hush comes over us, followed by a quiet sense of excitement and curiosity. Or perhaps we have found one of earth's gifts, a natural shelter from the harsh elements—we feel protected. The caves of Lascaux offered protection, a sanctuary and a canvas for an ancient world. And now, Lascaux is a place of delight and amazement. On the other hand, Plato's *Republic* taught us the myth of the cave, that something hidden, far from the light, resonates with secrets, things mysterious and even a little frightening.

More than 35,000 years ago primitive people were constructing caves or protecting the ones they found: Dwellings soon became places of safekeeping, burials, ceremonies, rituals; and, as Lascaux teaches us, caves could be art galleries. Some of our most reliable information about early humans and their relationship to their landscape and to the creatures of the earth has come from iconography in primitive caves. These ancient caves are found on all of the continents, even Antarctica. In Africa, the Namibian caves have become famous and have been utilized in modern times during both world wars for reliable water and nitrate supplies. During the American Civil War, bat guano from the Frio Cave in Texas was used as the chief ingredient of gunpowder. Now, in the 21st century, more caves are being mined than at any time in history, as we rediscover an ancient principle: The earth itself is a remarkable insulator from heat, cold, drying air and light, virtually impervious to subterranean shifting.

The earliest dedicated use of caves as wine storage is generally credited to the Etruscans around 800 B.C. Etruscan advances in civil engineering made extensive tunneling possible. The Romans who followed also saw the advantages of building underground; their catacombs became legendary—historical evidence suggests that they were also used for wine storage. Throughout Europe, during the reign of the Roman Empire, miles and miles of tunnels were excavated. The French utilized the abandoned crayères—limestone excavations left by the Romans—to store their wine. In the Champagne region of France, ancient stone quarries are used today for aging sparkling wines. In the Loire Valley, caves built in the Middle Ages by French noblemen now store wines. Although fewer in number, there are also medieval wine caves in use in Bordeaux and Burgundy.

In 1867 Jacob Schram cut the first wine cellar in Napa Valley in the side of Diamond Mountain. The cave was only a few yards long, limiting storage as the crew encountered rhyolite, a very hard rock. In 1881, with the help of Chinese laborers, excavations continued in a different location. Jacob's wife, Anne, supervised the construction, and by 1891 they had formed a massive underground network of caves.

Meanwhile, another German immigrant, Jacob Beringer, purchased the old Hudson Ranch just outside St. Helena, where he planted a vineyard and built a winery. In 1877 he hired 100 Chinese laborers to begin building his wine tunnels at a dollar a day—25 cents more than they had earned working for the railroad. With pick and shovel they excavated long tunnels. This work was dirty, difficult and dangerous. An unrelenting rain of falling dirt had to be carried out by hand in woven baskets.

More Chinese found work in Napa Valley digging caves and building rock walls, which are still standing today. Unemployed and disgruntled white men claimed that the Chinese were taking their jobs away, unwilling to admit that the Chinese did work they found unbearable. As contention continued to grow, the State Legislature passed a number of restrictive acts, and in 1882 the U.S. Congress passed the Chinese Exclusion Act, which prevented Chinese laborers from entering the states. The loss of the Chinese labor force signaled the end of cave building in Napa Valley, and by the 1890s no new caves were being created. The ensuing years brought phylloxera and Prohibition, and many of the old wineries closed and their facilities fell into disrepair and finally abandonment. The notion of digging a wine cave seemed to vanish.

For much of the wine industry's deep history, it has been known that a cool dark environment with constant temperatures between 55 and 60 degrees Fahrenheit is ideal for aging wine. In warm climates, such as northern California, the temperature inside caves averages about 58 degrees. Humidity levels between 70 and 90 percent are beneficial to reducing evaporation of wine. During the course of aging wine in 60-gallon barrels, a loss of four gallons or more per year can occur. In a humid wine cave these losses are reduced to about one gallon or less per barrel—a considerable savings for makers of premium wine.

As in all construction projects, much depends on budget and vision, but going into the earth brings in the unknown. Despite the intense study of the geology, an unexpected seam of mud or current of water or gargantuan boulder may be encountered, shifting the whole approach and design. Digging a wine cave, therefore, is part art, part science.

Some caves are simple, straight tunnels; some have graceful curves; others are vast underground, maze-like complexes exceeding 40,000 square feet. Several wineries are completely underground. A number of the caves have special underground chambers for wine libraries, dinners and events. These modern wine caves are like nothing built before.

The seeds of the modern wine-cave industry began to germinate in 1970 when the Swiss chocolate company Nestlé purchased Beringer Vineyards. Napa would soon burst with opportunities to dig.

Beringer Vineyards

Beringer Vineyards, established in 1876, is the oldest continuously operating winery in Napa Valley, and in 2001 the estate was placed on the National Register for Historic Places as an Historic District.

When Otto Beringer Jr. sold the winery to Nestlé in 1971, the winery was in need of modernizing. Guy Kay, the project director at that time, recalled that he realized a professional with tunneling experience was obviously needed when one of the employees, who was working in a section of tunnel, returned from lunch and found the area where he had been working half-buried from a cave-in.

John A. Bloom & Associates, the engineering firm hired by Nestlé for renovations, recommended a young civil engineer from San Francisco who they believed could handle the tunneling work. His name was Alf Burtleson.

In 1972 Alf and his crew were given a contract to make one tunnel section of the cave complex safe and usable. Guy Kay explained that he really didn't know if what they were doing was going to work, so as the crew finished a section, he would give Alf a new contract for another section. They proceeded in this manner with Alf taking out collapsing timbers, installing concrete footings, pillars and floors, incorporating steel arches and backfilling with gunite.

The configuration of the complex consisted of two parallel tunnels approximately 400 feet long that were connected by two cross tunnels. Several shorter tunnels or little rooms emanated off the major long runs.

The 1,000 linear feet of Beringer Vineyards' caves, picked out by Chinese laborers more than a century ago, are certainly not modern wine caves and have never felt the tooth of a roadheader. Their restoration by Alf, however, gave them new life and use.

Beringer Vineyards continues to age fine wines in the tunnels, and visitors safely tour them daily because of his work. When Fosters Brewing Group of Australia bought Beringer Wine Estates in 2000, winemaster emeritus Ed Sbragia and winemaker Laurie Hook continued developing Beringer's notable wines, thanks in part to the winery's century-old caves.

Cave Size: 13,000 square feet

Winery Specialties: Cabernet Sauvignon, Merlot, Pinot Noir, Chardonnay, Sauvignon Blanc, White Zinfandel

Roadheader, Dosco MK2A

Dale Wondergem and Gil Nickel, just prior to blasting the first tunnel at Far Niente.

1981
Alf Burtleson Construction began Far Niente's caves.

1982
To expand Chinese-dug caves at **Schramsberg Vineyards**, the Alf Burtleson crew used a Dosco MK2A Roadheader—a formidable piece of equipment weighing 30 tons with an extending boom, mounted with various rotating cutting heads. Invented in the 1940s, the roadheader was used by Welsh coalminers for its maneuverability. Today, these machines are the standard equipment for creating caves. Dale Wondergem took the controls and began grinding out wine caves.

1983
Storybook Mountain's 1890s cave portal was widened and modernized by Alf Burtleson Construction.

1984
Alf Burtleson Construction designed and created **Rutherford Hill Winery**'s cave.

Dick Graff and Phil Woodward were so pleased with their new cave at Carmenet that they asked Alf to build one at **Chalone** in Monterey. Tied up with the Rutherford Hill project, Alf suggested they consult with Dick Harding, the geologist on the Carmenet job. Harding put together a crew and blasted a small tunnel at Chalone. Unfortunately, the cave turned out to be above geothermal activity, and the expense of installing a cooling system for the cave was, ironically, needed.

Napa Valley Chamber Music Society first performed in a cave at S. Anderson.

1980

1976
International recognition showered down on Napa Valley after the famous Paris Wine Tasting of 1976. In blind tastings with all French judges, Napa wines not only won the top honors at this Judgment of Paris, with Winiarski's 1973 Stag's Leap Wine Cellars Cabernet Sauvignon and Grgich's 1973 Chateau Montelena Chardonnay, but also made up six of the 11 most highly rated wines.

1982
Alf Burtleson Construction mined out 15,000 cubic meters of rock in the steep hills of the Sonoma County side of Mt. Veeder. This large project represents the first completed modern wine-cave complex at a virgin site for **Carmenet Winery**, today known as **Moon Mountain Vineyard**. The cave, designed by David Sellers for the Chalone Group and led by the late Dick Graff, remains basically unchanged and has been in continual use.

1983
S. Anderson Vineyard's cave complex, with gothic ceilings, marked the first modern wine cave completed at a virgin site in Napa County. S. Anderson became the first to hold musical events in a wine cave here. The cave remained as originally created by the Alf Burtleson crew and was in continual use until the winery was sold to Cliff Lede in 2002.

David Auerbach, "The Improvisator," gave his first musical performance in a cave and declared that the resonance in the earth was a natural sound spa for the mind. He played a mountain dulcimer for the dedication of the cave at Carmenet.

Gil Nickel

Cave musician David Auerbach

S. Anderson

Moon Mountain (Carmenet)

1986
Alf Burtleson always considered saving valuable agricultural land for production a key benefit of wine caves. His company created **Newton Vineyards'** wine caves, the first to be directly under a vineyard high on Spring Mountain. It was also the first time Dale Wondergem used a laser to guide his wine-cave excavations.

1988
Alf Burtleson Construction created additional tunnels for **Sterling Vineyards** and new caves for **Folie à Deux Winery** and **Forman Vineyard**.

Phase Two of Newton Vineyards' cave undertaken by Underground Associates.

1989
Alf Burtleson Construction returned to two previous clients. At **Far Niente**, it created 15,000 square feet of new tunnels, while enlarging the original tunnel. At **Clos Pegase**, it created additional tunnels and the large underground room with a stage and art niches.

Dick Harding formed a company of three generations of hard-rock miners. Using dynamite, pick axes and shovels, they carved through limestone and schist to create **Ironstone Vineyards'** cave, the first in Calaveras County.

Underground Associates created a cave for **Dunn Vineyards**, Randy Dunn's winery. As the decade came to a close, 20 modern wine-cave complexes had been established. It was a pioneering time when no fire regulations or building permits were required, but that was all about to change.

1989

1985
The old, hand-dug tunnel at **Wente Sparkling Wine**, formerly **Cresta Blanca Winery**, was repaired and modernized by Alf Burtleson Construction.

Working with the San Francisco Museum of Modern Art, Jan Shrem sponsored an architects' competition to determine who would design his new winery, **Clos Pegase**. From a field of 96 entrants, the judges selected renowned Princeton architect Michael Graves, who was commissioned to build both a "temple to wine and art" at the base of a knoll and a home for Jan and wife Mitsuko at its summit. Within the knoll, 20,000 feet of aging caves would be excavated, including a cave theater, a dramatic setting for celebrations, presentations and special events.

Hans Faden Winery's charming small tunnel soon became the site of elegant dinners and is now known as "the wedding cave."

Rutherford Hill first hosted Carols in the Caves, featuring the music of David Auerbach.

1987
Alf Burtleson Construction began Phase Two of Far Niente, a project that marks contractor Daniel Bazzoli's entrée into cave floor finishing.

A new era began as a second cave-building company entered the valley. Alf Burtleson Construction was in demand, and prospective clients were learning that it might be a year or more before their projects could begin. Alf Burtleson Construction created caves at four new sites this year and added tunnels at Schramsberg Vineyards.

Alf Burtleson Construction created caves for **Anderson's Conn Valley Vineyards**, home of Eagles Trace Winery; **White Rock Vineyards**; **Sterling Vineyards**; and **Sinskey Winery**, as well as a test tunnel for **Chandon** that is now used for storage.

A joint venture—the British Brewing Company, Whitbread, Piero Antinori of Tuscany and the champagne house of Bollinger—hired Dick Petterson to be the general manager of **Atlas Peak Winery**, now known as **Antica Napa Valley**. Dick had a degree in engineering and a farm-boy approach to life that meant doing things for oneself. Dick was already sold on the idea of caves but not on the idea of waiting a year for Alf Burtleson Construction to build. Whitbread sent him to England to visit coal miners in operation, and upon return he leased a Dosco. Dick, his young vineyard manager Glen Salvia, and Jim Crowley—"a jack-of-all-trades fellow who was dynamiting rocks in the developing vineyards," as Dick recalled—constructed their own 30,000-square-foot cave system. The rock was in a strong matrix of lava and boulders that was so hard they did not need to apply shotcrete. Once the cave was completed, the Atlas Peak group sold the mining equipment to Glen Ragsdale and Russell Clough who had just started up their own business in the valley, but not before Jim Crowley took the roadheader over to the eastern regions of Napa County and created a small cave complex for **Moss Creek Winery**.

Not wanting to wait, the new **Pine Ridge Vineyards** decided to hire the new company **Underground Associates**, headed up by Glen Ragsdale and Russell Clough, who created 10,000 square feet of tunnels for the winery for their first job.

Daniel Bazzoli being observed by aspiring young cement workers.

Far Niente

One would never know that deep beneath stately oaks and manicured gardens covering the hill behind Far Niente winery, cellar workers tend their wine's development in a romantic, timeless space lined with 2,500 French oak barrels. This winery was founded in 1885 by John Benson, a California Gold Rush 49er and uncle of the famous American painter Winslow Homer. It prospered until the onset of Prohibition in 1919, when, like many wineries, it was forced to close. But even in disrepair, the winery was still a magnificent old stone structure set against one of those mid-valley knolls. A stone archway in the west wall of the cellar indicated that wine caves were to be chiseled into the solid rock that the building was set against. Unfortunately, Benson never saw these caves materialize.

In the late 1970s Gil and Beth Nickel arrived in the valley, purchased the old Far Niente winery and began a three-year restoration of the property. The couple realized that a cave would be a perfect solution to creating the additional space to age wine without the expense of adding stone buildings. Plus, and likely more important to Gil at this time, he could enjoy the intriguing and romantic notion of carrying through Benson's original plan. Gil was a charismatic man of joyful vision with the keen sense of finding the right people to guide his visions to fruition. Gil hired Alf Burtleson for the job, and little did the two men know that the Far Niente wine cave—the first to be constructed in North America for almost a century—would spawn a new industry in California wine country.

It was spring of 1981 in Napa Valley, and Gil was nervously keeping a close eye on the small crew creating the tunnel. Alf's wife, Mary, remembers, "Gil was wringing his hands down there as they were setting up, saying, 'Boys, don't knock down my building!'" Later, in his folksy Oklahoma style, Gil would tell how Alf won his confidence: "In those days they were doing it with dynamite, and I was real nervous about my old historic building. Just before they set off the first dynamite charges, Alf called me down there, and we went outside to one of the cornerstones of the buildings. Alf put a coin on edge and, honest to God, they put off the dynamite and the earth shook and a big cloud of dust and rocks came belching out from the back of the winery right on out through the front door, and that coin was still standing on edge when it was over! I put my arms around Alf and said, 'You're my man!'"

The wine cave began as a narrow, rather short tunnel dug that May. For the next 20 years the cave evolved as Dale Wondergem, the "roadheader artist" for Alf Burtleson Construction, ground out a vast underground maze of rooms and tunnels of varying sizes and shapes. The additional construction phases, carried out in '87, '89, '95 and 2000, have created a shining jewel in the array of wine caves today, elegantly merging function with form. The design was largely a result of the synergetic relationship between Gil and two young men, Dirk Hampson and Larry Maguire. Dirk joined Far Niente as assistant winemaker in 1982—the same year that winemaking returned to this historic property—and became winemaker in 1983. Larry joined the fledgling winery in 1983 and was charged with developing the winery's marketing and sales strategy. To introduce a worldview to their young staff, Gil and Beth began taking the team to Europe to visit the great wine estates. Larry recalls: "Our tour of the round barrel chai at Château Lafite inspired us. We realized then that we had a chance to do something very special with our caves so we took the challenge seriously. We always knew we needed a proper wine library, but it was driven home in '87 with our morning tasting in the Auxey-Duresses cellar of Madame Lalou Bize LeRoy's father and the tasting afterward at Domaine de la Romanée-Conti. The resulting design looks nothing like either place, but the spirit of the tasting with Lalou lives with me each time I'm in our library."

Bouchard Père et Fils in Beaune influenced Far Niente's rear-exit grotto. Visitors enter those caves, wander throughout the walls of the city of Beaune and end up in a grotto—a magical sensation. "We loved the brick cellar under Maison Louis Latour's Corton Grancey," says Larry. "You could look through archways to see barrels in another room. Our cave construction wouldn't accommodate a similar design, but Dirk's lighted niches brought some of the feel that we experienced in that cellar. Looking down our corridor with the niches you get the sense of small, interconnecting passages."

Dirk absorbed those early brainstorming sessions with Gil and Larry and took the lead in designing the cave where he would make Far Niente's wines. This elegant cave complex is a reflection of Dirk's concern for aesthetics and his enormous attention to every detail, including 15 separate utility systems, all of which make working and being in the cave a total pleasure. The octagonal wine library with its graceful domed ceiling, several 45-degree-angle tunnels, and the exquisite lighting throughout the caves are just some of the elements that evoke an enchanted atmosphere. The cave complex comprises more than a perfect setting to age the Estate Chardonnay and Cabernet Sauvignon wines. Within a separate special section of the cave is housed Dolce, the only American winery dedicated to producing a single late-harvest wine.

In 1997 Far Niente launched Nickel & Nickel winery as a separate brand devoted to producing 100-percent-varietal single-vineyard wines. This winery would be located on an historic 19th-century farmstead built by John C. Sullenger. The 42-acre vineyard property just northeast of Far Niente was situated on the flat valley floor and thus was unsuitable for caves. Understanding the value of going into the earth and wanting to preserve the historic integrity of the Queen Anne-style home and barns on the property, a 30,000-square-foot barrel cellar and press area was dug underground and connected to two aboveground fermentation barns. Dirk applied all his knowledge of underground environments and designed his dream facility within the limits of the flat land.

The project broke ground in June 2001, with Gil's nephew, Erik Nickel, a restoration specialist, as the construction manager. When the project was completed in the summer of 2003 the original look and appeal of the 1880s American farmstead was restored. A casual observer might not realize the property housed a cutting edge winemaking operation. Almost 30 years after establishing the first modern wine cave, Far Niente initiated another first for the wine industry. In 2008 the winery mounted nearly 1,000 solar panels on pontoons and floated them on the vineyard irrigation pond. This "Floatovoltaic" system suggests new considerations of the placement and structure of agricultural ponds.

Cave Size: 40,000 square feet
Cave Designers: Dirk Hampson; Gil Nickel; Larry Maguire
Cave Architect: Lail Design Group, Jon Lail, Doug Osborn, Chau Vu
Cave Contractor: Alf Burtleson Construction
Lighting Consultant: Jan Moyer

Winery Specialties: Estate Chardonnay, Estate Cabernet Sauvignon

Top: The Queen Anne-style Sullenger home at Nickel & Nickel has been completely restored.

Middle: A cut-and-cover barrel chai is situated under Nickel & Nickel's fermentation barn.

Bottom: The vineyard pond at Far Niente features an innovative "Floatovoltaic" system.

Right: A ginkgo-lined drive leads to Far Niente.

When Jack and Jamie Davies moved to picturesque Napa Valley in 1965, they purchased the abandoned yet historic Schramsberg winery, a dilapidated winery celebrated by Robert Louis Stevenson in *The Silverado Squatters*. The gardens were overgrown and the Victorian house was in disrepair, yet the extensive wine tunnels dug by Chinese laborers in the 1800s had stood the test of time.

The caves were still good from a structural standpoint. As the years passed, the tunnels began to fill with Schramsberg's beautiful Méthode Champenoise sparkling wine. By the time Alf Burtleson Construction was creating the tunnel for Gil Nickel at Far Niente, Jack was calling him to come up and discuss expanding the tunnels at Schramsberg Vineyards.

Alf saw immediately that conventional drill and blasting would be inappropriate, not only because of the proximity to all those bottles of sparkling wine, but also because the geology where they wanted to extend the caves was volcanic tuff, a type of rock consisting of consolidated volcanic ash ejected from vents during a volcanic eruption. It is one of the easier rock formations to grind through, yet it has an integrity and strength that can let it stand without shotcrete. Thus Alf leased a Dosco MK2A roadheader to create significant expansion to the cave complex.

The late Jamie Davies remembered the day it arrived: "At that time, it looked a little like something from outer space because it was a machine that was on tracks; it had very long tracks, like a tractor, but much more spaceship-looking somehow. To get it up here they had to lay planks on the roadway so as to not gouge out the road."

In these caves where the sparkling wine is made, there are no barrels, only bottles—over two million of them.

Inside the dark tunnels are cave rooms 13 feet wide, 13 feet tall and 45-60 feet long, in which it takes the cellar workers two weeks to stack 250,000 to 300,000 bottles of wine. Stacked deep in the earth the wine will age from two to six years or longer, depending on the style, before being touched again by human hands when the riddling process commences. From deep inside the darkness of the cave come rhythmic volleys of drumming, kindling a vision that somewhere down one of the tunnels a secret ritual is being conducted. There, cellar workers lift the sleeping bottles from the enormous stacks and rap them in fast patterns on hard rubber mats to loosen the yeast in preparation for the final riddling process.

Unique to this cave is a dedicated team of men, with an average tenure of more than 20 years at Schramsberg Vineyards, who have gone into the earth every day to work. This cellar crew of Felipe Martinez, Efren Torres, Ernesto Herera, Miguel Moreno, Isidro Ceja and Ramon "the Riddler" Viera—the true cave men—is the heartbeat of the Schramsberg Vineyards caves.

Daily, Ramon the Riddler moves throughout the vast cave like a honeybee in a garden hovering briefly from flower to flower gathering nectar. His hands deftly move up and down the bottles in racks, twisting the bottles one-eighth of a turn each day and every day for six weeks, working the yeasts gently into the neck in preparation for the final steps of making the sparkling wine. And always is Ramon's little boombox filling the chambers with his beloved classical music.

Jamie shared: "The cave, I think, goes back to our roots, and if you walk in a cave, there is an air of mystery about it. I think that back in the recesses of the mind somewhere you connect to those early beginnings of man. And you may not put a name on it, but it

creates an emotional sensation; it's romantic because of the shades of darkness and the cracks of light coming through and the lack of openness. What is there? What sleeps there? You're not sure where all of these passages go, and you're not sure what is going to be at the end of all of them. It stirs you. Caves are a place to create rituals and legends and traditions in family groups—sort of a sanctuary for meditation and privacy as well as a place for celebration, I'm sure. And that makes me think of a birthday dinner we did for Hugh Johnson that my friend Molly Chappellet was so involved in. I was the one who walked down with Hugh and took that left turn into the little crossbar section of the cave that Molly had transformed into a garden. I still almost tremble to think about it; it was such an emotional experience, just stunning."

Today Hugh Davies, who played in the caves as a child, continues the work and carries on the dream his parents, Jack and Jamie, who started together more than 40 years ago. He now has the pleasure of watching his own young children play in these caves.

Cave Size: 40,000 square feet
Cave Contractor: Alf Burtleson Construction

Winery Specialties: J. Schram Rosé, J. Schram Reserve, Blanc de Blancs, Blanc de Noirs, Brut Rosé, Crémant Demi'sec, Mirabelle, Mirabelle Rosé, Querencia, J. Davies Diamond Mountain District Cabernet Sauvignon

A surprise party for Hugh Johnson turned Schramsberg cellars into a garden, a study and a fairyland banquet hall. A flute echoing in the dark corridor led the guests from the garden study to a short concert of Handel's *Water Music*. Continuing the Pisces birthday theme on the dining table, fish bowls held tulips and goldfish with tall branches of Magnolia stellata reflected in each guest's mirrored pond. Candlelight lit up the front row of 250,000 sparkling wine bottles stacked in the alcove beyond.

Founded in 1972, Rutherford Hill Winery pioneered the development of California merlot. The grape growers who began this winery carefully studied the geography of the region and capitalized on climate and soil conditions that resembled those of Pomerol, the small but distinctive merlot-growing region of Bordeaux. And what a promising discovery that was. The land has borne plenty of fruit, namely the lush, purple-black grapes that have contributed so much to Rutherford Hill's success. By the early 1980s Rutherford Hill was making a considerable amount of wine.

With the creation of the tunnel at Far Niente and new caves up at Schramsberg and Carmenet recently completed, the buzz about caves was in the air. While the S. Anderson cave was in progress, Alf Burtleson was contacted by Bill Jaeger, managing partner of Rutherford Hill, and asked to design and create a cave to house the 6,500 barrels that were being warehoused in the valley. The owners wanted to use a pallet-stacking system going four barrels high. This required the design of tall tunnels with space for maneuverability of forklifts. It would be the most massive project at the time. The material through which the Rutherford Hill caves run was a mixture of strata from four distinctive geologic zones.

The first phase of cave construction ran from 1984 to 1985 and included two portals and six caves. It wasn't easy. Dale Wondergem recalls, "Not long into the project we hit fractured rock and lots of water and had to change directions. Then we ran into real soft material. When you are doing tunnels you have adequate means to support the face where you are working—if you are working a 13-foot-wide tunnel, you've got a bare area 13 feet wide by 13 and a half or 14 feet tall, or however tall it is. So you have a huge face that just stands there, and if you are in really soft material, that face wants to blow out, it wants to slough off, and usually when the face falls it takes part of the top with it. On our first four jobs the ground had been decent, and we had only cut a diameter that the machine could reach. Rutherford Hill was a big learning curve for all of us because the caves were so tall and we had to do them in stages. We had to do the top section, and then come back and mine out of the bottom in very difficult material. I wasn't using a laser in those days—just going by line-of-sight with my plumb-lines and measuring."

As the winery began using the finished caves, the two cellar workers, normally busy every week topping those 6,500 barrels, found they had very little to do. The wine wasn't evaporating in the cool, humid caves. The savings of approximately a case of premium wine per barrel for topping each year, plus rent fees and labor, allowed the winery to pay off the total cost of construction in two years. In a valley where information was shared readily, the economic advantages of caves were starting to make sense.

The second phase, from 1990 to 1991, included a series of short connecting tunnels, a back cave and a dining grotto for special events. The capacity of the cave was increased to house 8,000 French and American oak barrels. The entire system extends for nearly one mile and maintains an ideal, consistent storage environment of 59 degrees with up to 90-percent humidity. When the Terlato family of the Terlato Wine Group, Lake Bluff, Illinois, purchased the winery in 1996, they immediately began to apply their guiding principle: Quality is a way of life. The pursuit of excellence began with a comprehensive review of all aspects of the facility that resulted in significant enhancements.

Aesthetic improvements to the caves were begun in February 2000, including a fresh layer of shotcrete on the interior cave walls and an additional lighting system with sconces and chandeliers. The continuous attention to detail displayed in the construction and ongoing enrichments to the cave system exemplifies the commitment to quality of the Terlato family and underscores their dedication to excellence in all fields.

Cave Size: 40,000 square feet
Cave Designer: Alf Burtleson
Cave Contractor: Alf Burtleson Construction

Wine Specialties: Merlot, Chardonnay, Cabernet Sauvignon, Rosé, Merlot Reserve

Anderson's Conn Valley Vineyards, home of Eagles Trace Winery

Gus and Phyllis Anderson are pioneers in the modern wine-cave world as well as strong advocates of wine caves, having built two. In 1983 they purchased 40 acres of rural land in Conn Valley, a small valley within Napa Valley and, along with their son Todd and his wife, began development of Anderson's Conn Valley Winery and Vineyards. Within three years their new vineyards were developing well and they contacted Alf Burtleson to build a cave. There were only eight caves built at the time, but for the Andersons the decision to go into the earth was straightforward. Gus recalls, "The temperature and humidity in a cave are ideal for the storage of wine. We had a perfect place to put a cave and the cost was no more than it would be to build an aboveground storage building, which would require much more money to maintain." The simple design was dictated by the hillside, and by using side tunnels, the winery became more functional: "I didn't want just one long tunnel."

The design of the cave allowed for natural drainage by having a two-degree slope from the back to the front, as well as a two-degree slope from the walls to the drainage channels and a slope from the center of the tunnel sideways to the drainage channels. The concrete floor was so rough and poorly finished that Gus didn't think he could live with it. So, he had the floor tiled with pavers from Mexico, which has proved to be both functional and good looking.

The cave, having been built in the 1980s before regulations required two portals, is one of the few "dead-end" wine caves one will experience in the valley. The cave has such acoustical qualities that visitors can whisper at the end of the cave and be heard out near the entrance. This was most evident when the owners had a harpist play for their daughter's celebratory wedding reception. Thirteen years later with vineyards maturing and business successful, Gus, Phyllis and Todd needed to expand and had a second cave complex built on a facing hill above the vineyards. This one had two portals. By 2002 Todd had taken over the operation of Anderson's Conn Valley Winery, and Gus retired from making wine to concentrate on running the vineyards. It was less than a year before Gus realized how much he loved and missed making wine. So, at a time when most people his age were retired, he and Phyllis founded Eagles Trace, a winery dedicated to making small lots of great wine. The entire winemaking facility is in the cave.

Like an alchemist in his favorite laboratory, Gus finds the conditions of his old familiar cave ideal for creating his Eagles Trace Bordeaux-style wines. After early morning picking, the crew brings the fruit into the cave where it is crushed into the tank with the temperature at 50 degrees or cooler. Gus believes a long cold-soaking of the grape must, before the start of fermentation, encourages development as the grapes "get to know each other." As the fermented wine cools down over many weeks in the cave he feels he gets a better, softer tannin development before the wine goes to barrel. Gus makes three different wines that follow the footprint of three distinct areas of Bordeaux: Pomerol, Pauillac and Graves.

Cave Size: 3,000 square feet
Cave Designers: Alf Burtleson Construction; Gus and Phyllis Anderson
Cave Contractor: Alf Burtleson Construction

Winery Specialties: Cabernet Sauvigon, Merlot, Latitude 38, Pinot Noir

Pine Ridge Vineyards

In 1978 Gary Andrus and Nancy Andrus Duckhorn founded Pine Ridge within a narrow crease in the steep hills just west of Stag's Leap Wine Cellars. Within a decade the terraced vineyards were bearing fruit, and storage space for their wine was needed.

Limitation of available flat land combined with their travels in the wine regions of Europe pointed to the decision to build a wine cave. They were ready, but Alf Burtleson Construction was not—his company was in such demand that the project would have to wait in line more than a year. In 1987 serendipity struck.

Russell Clough and Glen Ragsdale had just arrived in the valley with visions of expanding their underground construction company into a new wine-cave business. When Pine Ridge decided to try the new company, Gary and Glen forged an instant connection and a lifelong friendship.

Gary became one of the first to incorporate spoils from the cave into vineyard formation. The vines grown on those "muck" soils have done well. Spoils were also used to line the property reservoir and provide road base during additional expansion phases in 1995 and 1999.

For Nancy, every day was an adventure. At one point early on they discovered a few flakes of gold high on a pillar. Dreaming of new possibilities elicited an impromptu "Go for it!" No more gold was found, but if one knows where to look, a large gouge is still clearly visible high along a side tunnel.

Baked eons ago by the heat of the magma plug forming the hill across the road at Stag's Leap Wine Cellars, warm colors of earth were something Nancy wanted to share; but the shale-like stone kept flaking off. One face was left exposed, and today, after more than 20 years, thin stalactites hang from the intersection of the shotcrete and exposed earth.

Nancy and Gary appreciated the storage function of their cave but also recognized early the appeal of caves for entertainment and hospitality activities. They had Underground Associates create a large tunnel space at the back of the cave to serve this need.

Not all the work to build a cave occurs inside the earth. With concern that it may be too cool for guests, radiant heating was installed. This required ventilation that necessitated navigating a machine high up the side of a steep hill to sink a 120-foot vent shaft. After the cave was finished they discovered it wasn't necessary since the warmth generated by guests drinking wine seemed just fine.

Over the years many people may have gotten their introduction to wine caves at Pine Ridge. The main room, 120 feet under the earth, continues to have a multitude of uses including chamber music and dances. Nancy relates good-naturedly, "The most notorious has probably been the party for my 50th—it was called a "Naughty Leather & Lace" party where a gathering of folks in their finest biker attire witnessed Gary driving a Harley down the main tunnel."

Going north on the Silverado Trail, you encounter a close view of the portal into the steep hill. It's easy to begin wondering what occurs in that hillside. In 1999 Pine Ridge changed ownership and continues the founders' tradition of using the caves to their full potential.

Cave Size: 37,500 square feet
Cave Designer: Lail Design Group, Jon Lail, Doug Osborn
Cave Contractor: Underground Associates

Winery Specialties: Viognier, Rosé, Chardonnay, Merlot, Cabernet Franc, Malbec, Cabernet Sauvignon, Bordeaux

When the Alf Burtleson Construction crew completed a simple yet beautiful network of caves in a hillside of white volcanic ash, White Rock Vineyards became Napa Valley's first working underground winery. With the exception of grape crushing, all aspects of winemaking occur inside the caves.

In 1977 Henri and Claire Vandendriessche set out to revive White Rock Vineyards, which is situated in the southern foothills of the Stag's Leap Range. A vineyard and winery had been established there in 1870 by Dr. J. Pettingill. The original stone winery still stands after being converted into a residence in the 1920s.

The family planted a 36-acre vineyard in 1979, putting 21 hillside acres in four Bordeaux varieties and 15 acres of chardonnay in the lowest and coolest sector of their valley. During this time, thoughts of a winery were naturally occurring in the minds of Henri and Claire. As the vines were maturing, the couple deliberated about where they were going to make their wine. Going into the earth was the logical idea to Henri, for he had a most intimate experience with caves; he was born in one.

With the impending invasion of northern France in 1939, Henri's family fled to the South of France. With Henri on the way—his mother was pregnant at the time—the family took refuge in Amboise, moving into a cave dwelling there. This is where Henri was born. Henri's godfather, who was living in the area, was a self-sufficient farmer living in a 17th-century manor house. Behind it were walls of limestone into which caves had been dug. There his godfather kept tools, grew mushrooms and, of course, kept his wine. Henri would always admire the man.

When Alf and Mary Burtleson met with Henri and Claire, there was an instant friendship. Mary recalls, "They knew what they wanted, and Henri just sort of sketched it out on a napkin."

Claire wanted a procession of scale in the caves, a differentiation between large and small sections. The rock was strong and the condition solid enough to leave the cave without shotcrete. The Vandendriessches wanted to have some sections lighter, reminiscent of the chalky caves in southern France, so Alf left them the equipment. They themselves applied a thin layer of shotcrete mixed with light pigments to create the desired effects.

The constant humidity and temperature of White Rock Vineyards' caves safeguard the beautiful fruit flavors in the wines, keeping them from drying out and becoming harsh in the barrel. After bottling, the red wines are aged in the dark and vibration-free caves until they are ready to be sold. Only upon release are they labeled, encased and shipped.

Family owned and run by Henri and Claire and their two sons, Christopher, the winemaker, and Michael, the vineyard manager, White Rock Vineyards is an exemplary business uniting family and earth.

Cave Size: 6,000 square feet
Cave Designers: Henri and Claire Vandendriessche; Alf and Mary Burtleson
Cave Contractor: Alf Burtleson Construction

Winery Specialties: White Rock Vineyards "Laureate" Cabernet Sauvignon, White Rock Vineyards Napa Valley Claret, White Rock Vineyards Napa Valley Chardonnay, White Rock Vineyards Napa Valley Cabernet Sauvignon

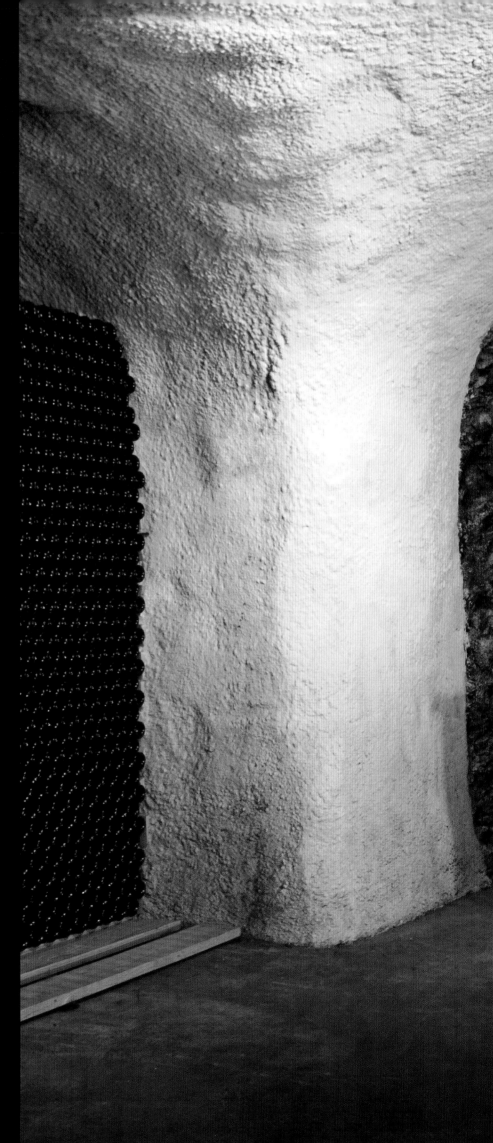

Murphys, California, is known as the Queen of the Sierras where many gold strikes were discovered. At one point there were an estimated 4,000 miners living on what is now part of the Ironstone Vineyards complex. When the Kautz family was exploring their options of building a winery on their ranch they knew the attributes of aging wine in caverns and wanted to utilize those natural benefits. Their first thought was to try to incorporate one of many open gold-mining shafts or tunnels left behind by the miners. When geologists analyzed those existing tunnels they determined that none was suitable enough to utilize. However, they discovered a solid rock mountain on the property that would lend itself to the creation of an ideal cavern.

The Kautz family contacted Alf Burtleson and learned he was too booked to send his crew over 150 miles from Napa Valley for this project, but Alf did suggest they contact Dick Harding, the geologist he worked with at Carmenet. Dick agreed to assist the family in forming their own mining company while his company, Earth Sciences, did the geological layout and design. "As we formed our own mining company to construct our caves," recalls Stephen Kautz, "there were many interesting characters that came and went. Many had colorful names: The Pig, The Mongoose and The Hatchetman. They came from Canada, Hawaii, South America and the Southeast. These included some of the 'old timers' who had worked the early gold and gem mines. They blasted, picked and shoveled their way through 10,000 square feet of limestone and schist to form the wine caverns. The project took 10 months to complete, and on many days, the miners would only make two to three feet of progress. The rock was so hard and difficult that the miners often said it was like blasting through iron. Thus, we became Ironstone Vineyards."

Stephen continues, "At one point, we had four generations of miners from one family on the project at the same time. They were a misfit group who lived underground most of their lives and loved it; and even though they didn't look the part, they were some of the most professional people to work with. They lived their lives blasting tunnels underground. One day, right after a shoot, there was

a commotion outside. The miners ventured out to see a good old fashioned fistfight taking place. I'm still not sure what started it, but when the crew foreman broke it up, they all shook hands and went back to work. Reminded me of something right out of a Western movie or a gold-rush book." Using the drill-and-blast method and not trimming out with a roadheader left the caves looking very natural. Because the caves are located in the Sierra Mountains, they benefit from annual snowmelt and water that moves down the Sierras through the natural strata in the rock. Since the wine caves were created, this natural process has helped to create stalactites in the caves.

The wine caverns were the first step in the creation of the Ironstone Vineyards winery and destination facility in Murphys and served as the facility's first tasting room. The winery complex sits above the caves and is architecturally designed to look like a stamp mill from the hard-rock mining days of the mid-1800s, falling in the timeframe of such mining throughout the Sierras. In addition to the winery and tasting room, a small museum is dedicated to the gold-rush era, filled with artifacts the Kautz family owns and has on loan. The Heritage Museum and Jewelry Shoppe showcases fine jewelry and a collection of recently found gold nuggets. On display is the world's largest specimen of crystalline gold leaf—a 44-pound treasure that was found in 1992 by the Sonora Mining Company. The winery building has a magnificent tasting room and gourmet delicatessen with a 42-foot stone fireplace and historic oak bar. The entire facility is used year-round for a variety of events, including a summer concert series in the outdoor amphitheater, cooking demonstrations in the culinary exhibition center, conferences, retreats and fairy tale weddings.

Cave Size: 10,000 square feet
Cave Designer: Earth Science
Cave Contractor: Ironstone Vineyards

Winery Specialties: Obsession Symphony, Xpression, Chardonnay, Cabernet Franc, Cabernet Sauvignon, Sauvignon Blanc, Shiraz, Verdelho, "Old Vine" Zinfandel, Merlot, Petit Sirah

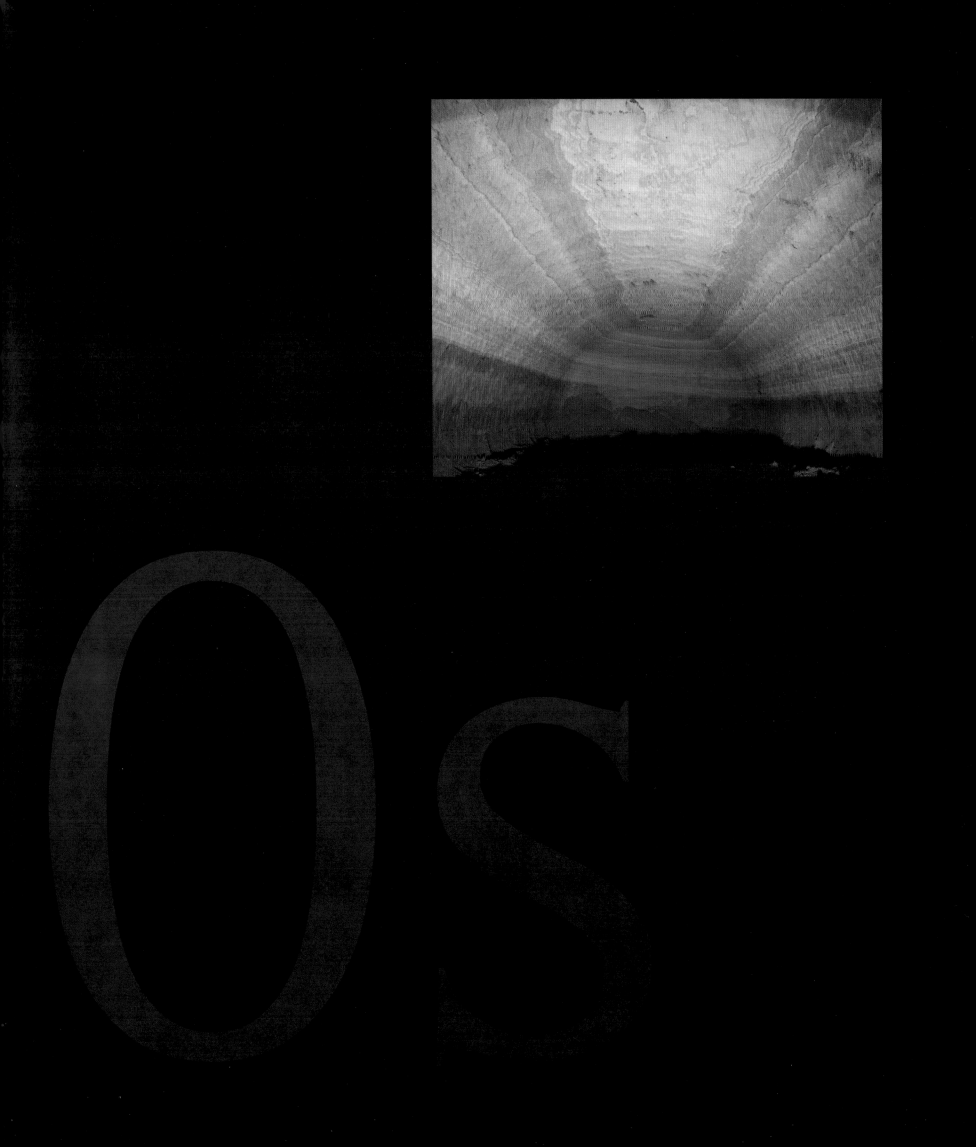

Quintessa vineyards

Rammed-earth walls of Long Meadow Ranch

1990

Alf Burtleson Construction returned to Rutherford Hill Winery to dig additional tunnels and a dining grotto for special events.

Underground Associates created two new cave systems: **Steltzner Winery** and **Kunde Family Estate**. Kunde's 35,000-square-foot system of caves, which took more than a year to complete, became the most massive project in Sonoma County at the time. During its construction there was a significant fire at the Americold Subterranean Warehousing facility near Kansas City, Missouri. The fire burned for four months, demonstrating the severe firefighting problems inherent in subterranean spaces: lack of easy access by fire-department apparatus, the difficulty of communicating in underground spaces and smoke management. Consequently, the construction of Kunde's cave triggered the first involvement of state and local fire marshals in developing fire codes for wine caves.

1992

Underground Associates was contracted for the original **Girard Winery** cave—the site now occupied by **Rudd Winery & Vineyards**—as well as **Gundlach Bundschu Winery**, the oldest winery in Sonoma County.

1994

Alf Burtleson Construction created new cave complexes for **Hafner Vineyard** and **Long Meadow Ranch**. Designed by award-winning architect William Turnbull, Long Meadow Ranch features an innovative use of the cave tailings, or spoilage. In creating the winery walls, rammed-earth expert David Easton screened the tailings and used them to construct one of the largest rammed-earth structures in North America.

Underground Associates created the first modern wine cave outside of California. **Archery Summit**, in Oregon, was established by the original owners of Pine Ridge.

1990

1991

Engineering geologist and tunneling consultant Scott Lewis of **Condor Earth Technologies** began his first wine-cave project, **Jarvis Winery**.

Alf Burtleson Construction built caves for **Livingston Moffett Winery** and **Shafer Vineyards** and began Jarvis Winery's. Two years in the making, Jarvis was the first totally underground winery and is still considered one of the most ambitious in terms of scale and concepts. The entire facility—more than 45,000 square feet of space for crushing, fermentation, barrel storage, lab, office and hospitality—is deep inside the earth.

1993

Alf Burtleson Construction, having finished at Jarvis Winery, returned to Sterling Vineyards for additional tunnels. The company created new wine caves at two facilities: **Araujo Estate Wines** and **William Harrison Vineyards & Winery**.

Glen Ragsdale became the sole owner of Underground Associates when his partner, Russell Clough, sold his interest and became a consulting professor at Stanford University. Underground Associates created cave complexes for **Schug Carneros Estate Winery** and **Rutz Cellars**.

Engineering geologist Scott Lewis, Condor Earth Technologies

Daniel Bazzoli traditionally places a liberty dollar in each of his floors.

Applying shotcrete

Alf Burtleson Construction: **Paoletti Estates Winery**.

Magorian Mine Services built its first cave, **Green & Red Vineyard**.

Nordby Construction established **Nordby Wine Caves** and created complexes for **Fisher Vineyards** and **Alexander Valley Vineyards**.

Underground Associates returned to two previous projects: Rombauer Vineyards, adding 12,000 additional square feet of tunnels, and Rudd Winery & Vineyards, where the complex was expanded to over 22,000 square feet. The company built new cave complexes at four additional sites: **Stag's Leap Wine Cellars**, **Hartwell Vineyards**, **BOND** and **Lancaster Estate**.

David Provost began creating wine caves under the name **Bacchus Caves** in one of the valley's original 19th-century caves at **Spring Mountain Vineyard**.

California State Fire Marshal's office developed minimum fire-protection and life-safety standards that were first adopted in the California Fire Code. These standards classify caves into three categories: barrel storage only, guided tours and tastings for a limited number of occupants, and hosted events for larger occupant loads.

1996

Alf Burtleson Construction: **Flora Springs**, **Screaming Eagle**.

Underground Associates created a large complex of caves at **Rombauer Vineyards**.

Rombauer Vineyards was **Brady Mitchell Construction**'s first finish-work project. From this point, Brady's company would work on more than 60 wine-cave projects.

1998

1999

1995

Alf Burtleson Construction returned to Far Niente to create another 13,000 square feet of caves and created caves at **Cuvaison** and **V. Sattui Winery**. V. Sattui Winery's caves are located within a hillside just south of Calistoga and preceded the construction of Castello di Amorosa.

Underground Associates returned to Pine Ridge to create an additional 15,000 square feet of tunnel storage and traveled to San Luis Obispo County for **Eberle Winery** and Santa Barbara County for **Cottonwood Canyon** to create the first wine caves in Southern California.

1997

Alf Burtleson Construction: **Truchard Vineyards**, **Miner Family Vineyards**.

Underground Associates: **Altamura Winery, Eagle & Rose Estate Winery, Keller Estate**.

Valhalla Vineyards in Roanoke, the first modern wine cave in Virginia, was created by **B-U Underground**.

1999

Anderthal Wine Caves created its first cave, which is now owned by **Fantesca Estate & Winery**.

Alf Burtleson Construction: **Vine Cliff Winery**, **Viader Vineyards**.

Magorian Mine Services: **A. Rafanelli Winery**, **Gloria Ferrer Winery**.

Nordby Wine Caves added new tunnels to both Robert Sinskey Vineyards' and Alexander Valley Vineyards' caves. Nordby created new caves for **Pietra Santa Winery**—the first wine cave in San Benito County—and **Chateau Montelena Winery**.

Underground Associates returned to two previous projects—Steltzner Winery and Pine Ridge Vineyards—to add significant new tunnels. The company also created new cave complexes at **Pride Mountain Vineyards** and **Black Sears Estate**.

Araujo Estate Wines

Jarvis Winery

William and Leticia Jarvis didn't set out to create the first and largest totally underground winemaking facility ever created when they purchased their property in the late 1980s. They simply thought that a vineyard might do well in their soils of well-drained volcanic origin, and that the altitude and closeness to San Francisco Bay brought coolness to the site.

For a brilliant, well-traveled and very successful Silicon Valley engineer and businessman, planting a vineyard would be done with intelligence and deliberation concerning choice of rootstocks, varietals, clones and management. It was no surprise that the grapes turned out to be of the highest quality.

"I had always been fascinated with geology and caves, so when it came time to build a winery I wanted to have it all underground," William says. "We didn't want to spoil the natural beauty of the area with large stainless-steel tanks and buildings." The couple traveled to all the important caves they knew of in the world seeking inspiration and ideas for their winery.

After a futile search for a cave architect, William decided to just plan it as they went along. The problem is that you cannot tell ahead of time what material you are going to run into underground. In two-million-year-old geology, there are lots of surprises. Once they had to totally change directions after drilling into loose soil that wouldn't support a cave. Another surprise was a little underground stream discovered during the tunneling. A hydraulic engineer was hired to develop this discovery into a source of humidity in the cave, something very desirable for barrel aging. The stream is cycled through an attractive waterfall to serve this purpose as well as to provide a calming effect.

From his travels and education, William understood the strength of the parabolic Venetian arch, which is critical in the support of the large chamber ceilings. He explains: "The Romans made extensive use of the arch in portals, bridges, aqueducts, temples and in the famous Roman Colosseum. The Roman semicircular arch is quite strong, but in terms of load bearing, it has a weak point at its top; the parabolic-shaped arch as employed in Venice does not have this weakness. It was used to beautiful advantage in the palaces of Venice. The parabolic arch can support nearly equal loads at all points. It is also more elegant."

Fortunately, at the time of construction, geotechnical engineers at the University of California had just made great progress in computer calculations for large underground spaces for testing nuclear bombs. Such calculations were required for safety and structural considerations since this cave must support the whole mountain above it without fear of collapse. The necessary computer modeling itself had also just become practical as a result of higher speed computers. As it was, it took geotechnical consultant Gregg Korbin more than two months of all-night calculations with UC Berkeley's most powerful computer to model and design the largest underground chambers.

Jarvis designed the primary tunnel in a circular pattern so that the winemaker and the lab would be close to all barrels of wine. Dimitri Tchelistcheff, Jarvis' winemaking consultant, planned all the interior winery equipment. Other caves emanate from and through the main tunnel. The fermentation gallery is 18 feet high and 26 feet wide, and each tank has an exhaust duct for removing carbon dioxide during fermentation. To help with air movement the tunnels all slope toward an exit, since carbon dioxide is heavier than air and settles downhill. The largest chamber in the underground complex, the barrel chai, is 80 feet wide with an arching ceiling almost 40 feet high unsupported by columns. It is used for barrel storage and rare-wine club events, as is another large room containing numerous giant amethyst geodes the Jarvises have collected in their travels.

Throughout the cave's design there are many arches, subtly echoing the parabolic form. With the help of local artist Jim Gangwer and other area artisans, the cast-bronze doors, brass wall sconces, arched alcoves and fiber-optic chandeliers have all added to the mystique and beauty of the cave.

With the vineyards located on the same property and close to the cave, once the grapes are picked they do not to have to sit in picking lugs and deteriorate. They are delivered directly to the cave for immediate crushing followed by fermentation. The close proximity of the vineyard allows the winemaker to collaborate daily with William and the vineyard manager on all the decisions including harvesting, as timing is critical for the finest wines. In short, the cave winery is the final step in the production of fine wine. William believes that Dimitri has made the best wines of his career in the constant low-temperature environment of this deep cave.

William also good-naturedly shares that his winery crew adapted quickly to working underground eight hours a day. "When visitors come we ask them how the weather is outside. And my long-time staff members relish the fact that their skin remains soft and smooth in the cool, humid conditions."

Cave Size: 50,000 square feet
Cave Designers: William Jarvis; S. Scott Smith, Sasaki Associates
Geotechnical Engineers: Gregg Korbin; Tor Brekke; Jon Kaneshiro
Engineering Geologist and Tunneling Consultant: Scott Lewis, Condor Earth Technologies
Civil Engineers: Dick Dokken; Bill Phillips
Cave Excavators: Alf Burtleson Construction; Bill Ley Construction

Winery Specialties: Cabernet Sauvignon, Lake William Cabernet Blend, Cabernet Franc, Merlot, Chardonnay, Petit Verdot, Tempranillo

Above: Dimitri Tchelistcheff

Right: The barrel chai is large enough to hold all the aging barrels or serve as a grand chamber for an elegant ball.

Above: The cave entrance is nestled in the hills above Napa.

Top Left: Large oak cuves have been imported from Cognac, France.

Left: The fermentation gallery includes the latest rotary fermenters as well as upright tanks.

Facing Page Top: A waterfall in the main corridor humidifies barrels in all parts of the cave.

Facing Page Bottom: Up to 10 visitors can gather in the tasting room.

When Bart and Daphne Araujo acquired the Eisele Vineyard in 1990, their goal was simply to be great stewards of the land and let the land speak. It certainly does in their vineyard and in their natural rock cave.

Their original winemaker, Tony Sotor, was keen on the idea of having a cave and took them to see different profiles of caves that were being built soon after they acquired the property. Daphne explains, "We visited Ric Forman's cave and loved its proportion. Only 10 and a half feet high—rather than the standard 12 or 13 feet—makes it feel just so much more intimate. We thought the most wonderful cave was the S. Anderson cave with its natural rock. And when we started ours, it didn't occur to us that we would have exposed stone. It was serendipitous."

For Daphne, with her landscape architectural background, creating a wine-aging facility that would not be seen was very appealing.

Araujo's cave is one of the few since the 1990s to receive a variance from engineering geologist and tunneling consultant Scott Lewis stating it could stand without shotcrete reinforcement. The rock was so solid that there were no cave-in delays and the crew didn't have to stop each day to apply shotcrete—they just kept drilling. Thus, the majority of this cave is pure exposed rock instead of concrete. Walking through the tunnels is indeed like being inside the living earth. When touching the walls, your fingers make direct contact with whatever energies occur in that substratum where roots exist.

Daphne beams when recalling the beginning: "Dale, with his ever-present smile, just took his little spray can of orange paint and painted an arch on the side of the hill and by the end of the day was 10 feet in where solid rock used to be. At the end of each day after that, there would be this face of solid rock wall where he had stopped. It looked very much like a mural or a cave painting. It was a thrill, a gift to see. It went really fast. There wouldn't have been a cave without Alf Burtleson and Dale Wondergem. Dale is such an artist and so skillful with that giant machine. Alf was the most wonderful

man to work with. Bart and I have built a lot of things in our lifetimes, and we both agree that this was the most special project. Alf was just a superb general contractor—so knowledgeable about caves, so anticipatory."

This property has been under vines since the 1880s when people discovered it was good vineyard land. It has the drainage of Simmons Canyon Creek running right through it. "This is really quite a special thing for a vineyard to have such energy flow," says Daphne. "The very rocky, river-bottom type of cobble puts a good stress on the vines, contributing to a great wine. So with our farming and our cave, we were looking for all the ways we could build on the terroir. Not to take anything away but to reinforce what we already had."

They couldn't do this by putting chemical fertilizers in the ground or spraying them on the vines. Through consultations with Amigo Bob Cantisano, the vineyards were certified organic by 1999. Seeking to deepen and refine their agricultural practices the Araujos began studying Biodynamic methods. A chance meeting with an old acquaintance, Jeff Dawson, an expert in the field, resulted in his guiding the Araujo vineyards to Biodynamic certification in 2001.

The grapes from the vines grown in these carefully tended vineyards never leave the property. After they're harvested and vinified in the winery at the entrance to the cave, they go into that hill to age and develop in an optimal place that resonates so clearly the rhythms of the earth and the principles of their farming.

Cave Size: 12,500 square feet
Cave Designers: Araujo Family; Alf Burtleson; Dale Wondergem
Cave Contractor: Alf Burtleson Construction
Engineering Geologist and Tunneling Consultant: Scott Lewis, Condor Earth Technologies
Concrete Floors and Library Bins Contractor: Daniel Bazzoli
Metalworker: Jim Austin

Winery Specialties: Estate Cabernet Sauvignon, Estate Sauvignon Blanc, Estate Syrah, Estate Viognier

Each year the Keller family has one special family party. Guests from all around the world are greeted at the winery with a glass of rosé. Once they have all gathered, a mariachi band leads everyone through the cave with the acoustics creating a spectacular sound. Most of the guests are unaware of the actual triumph in that walk through the cave that Ana Keller, the director and daughter of its founder, calls "the soul of the winery."

The winery was originally founded by Arturo and Deborah Keller and is the southernmost winery in the Sonoma Coast appellation, the first to be established in the Petaluma Valley. Keller Estate specializes in creating artisan, handcrafted pinot noir, chardonnay, pinot gris and syrah.

The cave came first, before Keller Estate had an actual winery. During the 2000 and 2001 vintage, a temporary crush facility was set up outside the cave on a concrete pad, where the fruit was fermented, moved to barrels and stowed in the cave for fermentation. The Kellers were adamant that all of the Keller Estate wines be produced on site. The winery was designed to fit the cave. It is split into two main sections to allow separation of chardonnay from pinot noir and syrah giving each the special conditions of temperature and humidity needed. The cave also has two alcoves where troublesome barrels can be monitored.

Construction of the 450-foot curving tunnel began in 1997 and took more than a year to complete. Taking into account all the massive complicated caves they have constructed in their history, Glen Ragsdale and Graham Wozencroft of Underground Associates consider this relatively small cave their toughest job. Imagine that: their toughest job.

This was the type of project where the roadheader was useless. The crew used shovels, pneumatic spades and a small excavator to remove the earth. Metal plates and breast-boards were used, supported by timbers, to prevent the face from sloughing off. On a good day, they could advance a mere three feet and install steel arches and shotcrete.

It wasn't the hardness of rock or concealed boulders that made the work difficult, but just the opposite. The ground in this ancient Tolay plateau is clay, and once the tunneling begins, the tension holding the soil is reduced and the ground begins to creep. The ground actually moves. That was the most challenging issue. In addition, the clay had a high water content.

"We had to revert to hand work," recalls Graham. "We were knee deep in mud all day long. There was a point where we just wanted it to end, but we just had to struggle on." The team made a curve, but weren't even sure they could push it to the end. "Any member of our crew who wasn't in shape when we started certainly was when we finally finished."

To reach the cave today, guests enter the elegant and spacious winery, which was designed by Ricardo Legorreta and constructed out of limestone quarried from the beds of the Yangtze River. Visitors are offered a beautiful shawl to wear as they proceed through the cave to the hospitality room. In its stillness and simple beauty, no detail belies what it took to build it.

Cave Size: 5,000 square feet
Cave Designers: Bill Rummonds & Associates; Arturo Keller
Cave Contractor: Underground Associates
Engineering Geologist and Tunneling Consultant: Scott Lewis, Condor Earth Technologies
Winery Architect: Ricardo Legorreta

Winery Specialties: Keller Estate Precioso Pinot Noir, Keller Estate Precioso Chardonnay, Keller Estate Rosé

Keller Estate's winery is made of limestone quarried from China's Yangtze River basin and recycled stone blocks that were salvaged from ancient buildings before the construction of the Three Gorges Dam that flooded 13 cities, 140 towns and 1,350 villages.

BOND, in its essence, is the covenant and shared commitment to produce only the best expression of the land. The enduring vision at BOND is the establishment of a stable of Napa Valley thoroughbreds—ultimately six cabernet sauvignon-based wines—diverse in geographic representation and Grand Cru in quality. Deep inside its cave, this rigid propulsion is seen; each wine, in fact, has its own cellar within the cave where the development of individual character and singular expression of place occurs.

The soil here is fantastic for growing merlot, yet for cave digging, it's some of the worst. Construction on BOND's cave began in October 1997 but, due to the extremely difficult ground, progressed at only about two feet per day—the cave was not completed until June of 2000. The soil is comprised of highly fractured rock, with clay platelet layers trapped between the fractures. For growing grapes, it has at the same time a perfect match of water-holding capacity and good drainage. But for a roadheader grinding a 13-foot-diameter face, the story is a little different.

During the process, Underground Associates had excavated several feet in when small rocks began to crumble down from the ceiling, creating large, gaping holes above. The crew soon found themselves stopping to stabilize these sections, pumping concrete into the void created by the falling rocks. Eventually they eliminated big machinery entirely, resorting to hand digging much of the cave using pneumatic spades. The spoils were recycled, spread out as road-base on the property prior to paving.

In design, the main part of the cave is circular with three tunnels emanating like spokes from a central room toward the perimeter. The circumference, at about 375 feet, can store some 1,000 barrels. Winemaker Bob Levy explains the design: "We wanted a circle to accomplish three things. Firstly, we could keep the distance traveled from the fermentation rooms down to a minimum; everything could be stored closer to the tanks. Secondly, by pure geometry, a circle has no dead ends, so we eliminated any dead air space. And thirdly, we could store the wine from six different properties in segregated areas. These three spokes, plus each section of the perimeter divided by each spoke, gave us the six zones we were looking for." This wheel-like design also gives a completely different sense and feel than a straight line with long rows of barrels.

There are 12 different zones in the cave where the temperature can be controlled separately, to heat or to cool, in order to accomplish better uniformity of climate as well as to help induce malolactic fermentation in the barrels. All of the heating and cooling is done with radiant tubing in the floors, where cold or hot liquid can be sent through, adjusting the temperature as necessary, while eliminating unwanted air movement in the cave itself. Air movement is designed into the cave, but at a very low volume, adjustable as desired.

"For humidity control," says Bob, "we rely on the natural ability of the earth to act as a sponge, drawing and releasing moisture at different times of the year." And this is the essence of cave design: Nature has an equilibrium that she persistently seeks, and to get the best wines out of the earth, we must trust our natural environment.

Cave Size: 10,000 square feet
Cave Designers: Bill Harlan; Bob Levy; Lail Design Group
Cave Contractor: Underground Associates

Wine Labels: Melbury, Quella, St. Eden, Vecina, Pluribus

Spring Mountain Vineyard

Spring Mountain Vineyard is an iconic wine estate with deep roots in Napa Valley's winegrowing history. Three contiguous 19th century vineyards comprise the 845-acre estate, purchased by Jacob E. Safra a century later. Each historic piece of the estate contributes to the diversity of the vineyard as a whole—its topography, elevation, soil type and climate—and ultimately to its wines.

Crowning the property at 1,600 feet above the valley floor is La Perla, planted in 1873 by Charles Lemme and expanded by the Schilling Spice family. The German-born Lemme built a redwood and stone winery that stands today as a "ghost" winery, along with much of its original farming equipment. Lemme is credited with planting the first cabernet sauvignon vines on Spring Mountain, a prophetic choice as this regal variety is now synonymous with Spring Mountain.

Just below La Perla lies Chateau Chevalier, a magnificent stone winery with original stained glass created in 1891 by its founding vintner, Fortune Chevalier.

Next door to Chevalier is Miravalle, established in 1884 by Tiburcio Parrott, a gentleman farmer who grew grapes, olives, citrus, roses and tobacco. His grand Victorian, Villa Miravalle, is beautifully restored and overlooks the valley. In 1885 Parrott tunneled into the hillside behind his home to create a wine cave in which to store his award-winning claret.

As Parrott was quite a colorful character, many entertaining stories about him have survived. One such story tells of an escapade involving his cave. During one of his famous dinner parties at Villa Miravalle, and perhaps under the effects of a "brandy haze," he began bragging about the ease of cave excavation. To prove his point, he led his guests to the cave-in-progress for a demonstration. He boldly lit a stick of dynamite, tossed it into the tunnel and collapsed its deepest recesses. Despite this bit of folly, the 90-foot-long tunnel was completed and stands today. Its rounded ceiling was formed of concrete and still shows the rustic marks of the wood planks used to shape its contours.

Just over a century after Parrott, Lemme and Chevalier planted vines on the steep slopes of Spring Mountain, Jacob E. Safra combined the properties, naming it Spring Mountain Vineyard.

His appreciation for wine, history and beauty led to a total revitalization of the newly formed estate during the 1990s. He chose to grow his vines sustainably, with the least impact to the environment, wildlife and community. His vision affected everything, from how the vineyards were planted to the restoration and preservation of the many historic buildings.

Of primary importance was the production of one signature wine from his estate, a red wine that would express the truest nature of the vineyard in an elegant, European style. In 2000 he put his personal mark on the wine, naming it Elivette. Safra's expanded vineyard holdings were producing rich, concentrated mountain wines that required a patient regimen in French oak barrels. He needed more space for aging, but believed that a barrel building would mar the natural landscape and was not environmentally sound. He decided to build upon Parrott's cave.

Excavation began in 1998 and took two and a half years to complete. Serpentine rock and extremely wet conditions created by natural springs made the work slow and dangerous. To preserve the original cave meant that the point of entry into the hillside, and where all the cave tailings were brought out, was far away from the original cave, yet ultimately destined to meet it. Halfway through the project, a re-design for stability was necessary, and rather than face further delays, the garden and vineyard workers pitched in to help. They learned how to weld and install steel arch supports. They installed a special waterproof liner and hand-trowelled the cave's plaster walls. On the day the crew pushed through to connect the new and the old cave, the story of Parrott and the dynamite was told and retold. Would there be some wine bottles found in the space separating the two caves? In the end, nothing was found, but the joining of the old and new caves was complete.

The new cave resembles the shape of the original cave, yet is unusually wide and dramatic. Its smooth walls are pigmented with soft color, and lighting provided by simple copper sconces is warm and welcoming, and the cave maintains a consistent temperature that ages the estate wines to polished and integrated perfection. An expanse of matched French oak barrels stacked only two high—for easy access by winemaker Jac Cole, vineyard manager Ron Rosenbrand and the rest of the crew—makes the cave both beautiful and practical.

High atop Spring Mountain Vineyard, a swing hangs from the limb of an ancient oak tree. It was placed there to honor a vineyard foreman, Francisco Alcantar, who had tended the vineyards for 30 years. From his swing, looking down the convolutions of steeply terraced vineyards, one can glimpse the cupola on the Villa Miravalle. The circle of winemaking is striking: Soil, vines and grapes are meticulously tended, and the wine returns to the cave below. And this unique cave—both very old and very new—bears the enormous weight of the vineyards above it.

Mr. Safra wanted the new cave to echo the beauty of the wines, but it does much more than that. The cave reflects the broader intent of the estate as a whole: to build upon historic legacy with an eye toward a bright, sustainable future.

Cave Size: 22,000 square feet
Cave Contractor: Bacchus Caves
Engineering Geologist and Tunneling Consultant: Scott Lewis, Condor Earth Technologies

Winery Specialties: Elivette, Cabernet Sauvignon, Syrah, Syrah Co-Ferment, Pinot Noir, Sauvignon Blanc

Above: A tribute to Napa Valley's past, Villa Miravalle serves as a venue for winery activities and special events.

Right: From Francisco Alcantar's swing, the cupola is visible.

Previous Pages: Chateau Chevalier is nestled in the undulating vineyards.

Page 103 Top: La Perla is the highest historic structure on the property.

Page 103 Bottom: Just before bud break, Spring Mountain invites sheep to graze on the cover crop, reducing mowing needs.

"In the center of the cave, illuminated by soft light, a Foucault pendulum is suspended above a quartzite floor whose patchwork pattern evokes visions of the earth when viewed from the heavens. The Round Room is the 'beating heart' of the cave, where the pendulum serves as a metaphor for the passing of time, and the aging of wine," shared Warren Winiarski, founder of Stag's Leap Wine Cellars. "The cave worked well with my lower alcohol winemaking style. The environment is humid, full of aqueous vapors, so the aqueous part of the wine does not evaporate but the alcohol does. Fundamentally it is the vineyard that makes the wine, but the cave helps the proportions of the elements. The cave environment is a little taxing, though, as the need for cleanliness and air freshening is paramount in the humid, dark conditions."

When the winery was started, there was no master plan. No two buildings have an identical axis; they're all pitched to each other and grew up like a Mediterranean village. The buildings themselves were designed to accommodate the site's extant trees and boulders. Each building was tilted and twisted a bit to hug the hillside in order to save land.

Warren related: "When we acquired the FAY vineyard, it became apparent that we would need more space to age our estate wine. We began contemplating the idea of building a cave and learned from consultants that the geology of the site revealed an anomaly in the normal valley soils." Geologically Napa Valley is located in the Great Valley Sequence with underlying Franciscan Terrane, neither of which exhibits igneous rock. However, the rock at Stag's Leap Wine Cellars was a magma plug of extremely hard igneous rock that had uplifted eons ago. "It was something you couldn't dig into; you had to blast and then dig out. Drill and shoot was something Underground Associates was equipped to do, so we chose them."

Underground Associates' plan was completely orthogonal. Each of the intersections was a perfect 90 degrees from the tunnel that preceded it. It was a grid. "If you look at Chicago, for example, from the air, it appears to be a grid; there are few diagonals. But if you look, for example, at London from the air at night, it is a series of centers that have been connected over time. It's comprised of little villages and cow paths that connected the villages; for every right angle there are 25 diagonals each radiating from centers that became connected over time. It's irregular," explained Warren.

"Our daughter Julia questioned why, if our blocks of vineyards and wines were all so different, should all the caves be the same. Why not have different sizes and different angles instead of having this perfectly orthogonal floorplan? Everyone in the family accepted that; we were already in that mode from what we had done on the surface. So we duplicated that Mediterranean village-like organic structural element below ground as well. Also, when we started to dig the face on the exterior, everyone said that we had to shotcrete this material because, as hard as it is, when it gets exposed to air and weather it crumbles, and we would be left with crumbled rock along the base."

There was a little drama going on in that rock, which was discovered when the drilling began. The tree roots that grow above the rock can work themselves into soft places within it, so the trees are actually growing out of it. And the vines can live in the soil that comes from it. Warren wanted to expose that drama as something interesting for people to think about—for them to see the bits of root from long-gone trees, to see the process that creates the soil. The cave structure was designed to tell that story. The idea of covering it with shotcrete would have meant that the story would be lost.

Warren continued: "I don't know what led me, but one day looking through *Architectural Digest* I saw the work of Javier Barba in the Mediterranean Islands. He had integrated a building with the stone that was already there in an elegant, simple gesture, and I said, 'That's the man.' We invited him to come out, and Javier grasped the opportunity. He and our son Stephen talked about how they might leave that wall exposed as an alternative to shotcrete, and they developed some ideas about a wire mesh to hold back the crumbling, spalling rocks as they weathered. The rock bolts holding

the mesh were fitted with nuts shaped like stars and moons as an astronomical theme began to emerge. We refer to this structure over the entrance as The Arcade."

Julia made the fundamental revision to the original orthogonal plan. She was thinking again of the Mediterranean village idea, this time with a balcony overlooking a piazza—a center where all the streets converge from different directions. She wanted a place that would be sort of like that, and this became the Round Room, the construction of which required almost twice the vertical dimension to provide the structural strength. "Since we had this height, I thought why not put a pendulum here," Warren related. "The whole idea of time then took hold because we don't see the passing of time in the cave. It takes something at rest and something in motion to be able to know that time is passing. There is no sun, there's no moon, there are no stars, there's no cycling. The pendulum became a metaphor for the passing of time." Then Javier designed the curved irregular floor, resembling the earth under the stars. Feldspar from the stone in the vineyards was added to the cement and gave a sense of stars. Javier created the frothy light by designing sconces of punched copper that resemble comets.

According to Warren, "One thing led to another, ideas grew from ideas. It was a very collegial and contributory process, with many thoughts and hands and minds working together."

When the 1973 Stag's Leap Wine Cellars Cabernet Sauvignon took top honors at the famous Paris tasting of 1976, the winery vaulted into the ranks of the world's most noteworthy cabernet producers and placed Warren Winiarski among the world's most respected winemakers. Over the years these wines have become some of the most highly regarded and collectable. In 2007 a partnership between Ste. Michelle Wine Estates and Marchesi Antinori proudly accepted the stewardship of Stag's Leap Wine Cellars and its legacy.

Cave Size: 40,000 square feet
Cave Designers: Warren Winiarski and family; Javier Barba; Graham Wozencroft
Cave Contractor: Underground Associates
Engineering Geologist and Tunneling Consultant: Scott Lewis, Condor Earth Technologies
Cave Finish and Floors Consultants: Brady Mitchell Construction; Glenn Baker, Hamelton Stone Work

Winery Specialties: CASK 23 Cabernet Sauvignon, S.L.V. Cabernet Sauvignon, FAY Cabernet Sauvignon, ARTEMIS Cabernet Sauvignon, ARCADIA VINEYARD Chardonnay, KARIA Chardonnay

Fantesca Estate & Winery

Fantesca Estate & Winery, owned by Duane and Susan Hoff, is located above St. Helena on Spring Mountain and overlooks the southern vista of the prestigious winemaking district. Separating the winery from the family estate is a working cave where Fantesca ages its award-winning wines.

The Fantesca property was originally in the dowry of Caroline Bale when she married Charles Krug in 1860. Even then, it was recognized as prime mountain vineyard land. In 1889 a cabernet from this property, made by Hannah Weinberger, one of the earliest female winemakers, won one of the first awards for a wine from Napa Valley.

The cave was constructed in 1999 by Anderthal Wine Caves and is ideally built into the side of the mountain where the volcanic rock face is rumored to have once been a stone quarry. The cave stretches 280 feet across the 53-acre property. Two short 40-foot tunnels extend off the main tunnel at 90-degree angles near the middle of the cave, providing great aging facilities for Fantesca's wines and those of its custom-crush clients. "And, it certainly makes for an easy commute to the office everyday—from the house, through the cave, to the winery. It doesn't get much simpler than that," says proprietor Duane Hoff.

The Hoffs, college sweethearts and former senior executives from Minneapolis, were drawn to the property to pursue their dream of creating a family business where their two children could get involved in everything from harvesting the fruit to choosing the wine label. Even better, their son and daughter will know they had a hand in making the wine that will be served at their weddings someday.

In 2008 legendary winemaker Heidi Barrett joined the team to help create sexy, smart and unpretentious wines—all in the name of Fantesca, a fun-loving frolicking female in an Italian traveling comedy troupe during the Renaissance.

Cave Size: 5,000 square feet
Cave Contractor: Anderthal Wine Caves

Winery Specialties: Cabernet Sauvignon, Chardonnay, Petit Verdot, Pinot Noir

Jerry Seps shares his cave at Storybook Winery with guests on the Napa Valley Museum's first wine-cave tours.

2000

Alf Burtleson Construction returned once again to Far Niente for the final phase to this work spanning 20 years. The company also built a small cave complex at **von Strasser Winery**.

Magorian Mine Services built a large, totally underground winery for **Staglin Family Vineyard**.

Nordby Wine Caves: **Stag's Leap Winery**.

Underground Associates returned to Rombauer for more tunnels and worked on caves for **Chapin Family Vineyards** and **Neal Family Vineyards**.

2002

Alf Burtleson Construction returned to Flora Springs Winery & Vineyards and Ladera Vineyards to add new caves.

Nordby Wine Caves: **Justin Vineyards & Winery, Galante Family Winery, Williams Wine Cave, Nicholson Ranch**.

Magorian Mine Services: **La Jota Vineyard Co.**

Underground Associates: **Quintessa, Constant Diamond Mountain Vineyard**.

California Wine Caves: **Caldwell Vineyard and Winery, Gold Hill Winery**.

2004

Alf Burtleson Construction: **The Napa Valley Reserve, Ovid**.

Bacchus Caves: **Baldacci Family Vineyards**.

Nordby Wine Caves: **Venge Vineyards**, formerly **Rossini Ranch, Niebaum-Coppola Winery**.

Underground Associates: **Sodaro Estate Winery**.

Hawks & Hawks: **William Cole Vineyards**.

California Wine Caves created **Chinnock Cellars'** cave and worked on additions at Saracina Vineyards.

2000

2001

Bacchus Caves: **Benziger Family Winery**.

Hawks & Hawks undertook its first wine cave, **Frazier Winery**.

Magorian Mine Services: **Ferrari-Carano Vineyards & Winery, Vineyard 29**.

Nordby Wine Caves: **Amizetta Vineyards, Reverie Winery, Byington Vineyard & Winery**.

Underground Associates broke ground at **Palmaz Vineyards**, the world's largest wine-cave project, which took six years to complete. The company also created caves for **O'Shaughnessy, Montagna Napa Valley, Phelan Vineyard** and **Lawrence Winery**.

Alf Burtleson Construction: **Sloan Estate, Bryant Family Vineyard, Ladera Vineyards**.

California Wine Caves: **Toogood Estate Winery**.

Anderthal Wine Caves created **Saracina Vineyards**—Mendocino County's first wine cave—and **Robert Young Estate Winery's** cave.

Steven Moore Construction created its first cave, which is now known as **Lookout Ridge Winery**. The winery is especially celebrated for its Wine on Wheels program.

Steven established **Moore Family Winery**, creating a cave system that he built on for the next eight years.

2003

Bacchus Caves: **Bella Vineyards**.

Alf Burtleson sold his company to Jim Curry but continued to serve as a consultant. The company made new caves for **HALL Wines** and **Jericho Canyon Vineyard**.

Magorian Mine Services: **Hanzell Vineyards**.

Nordby Wine Caves: **Twisted Oak Winery, Catacula Lake Winery**.

Underground Associates: **Bill Smith Winery**.

Steven Moore Construction: **Calistoga Ranch**.

Palmaz Vineyards

Some of the Underground Associates crew during Palmaz construction.

CADE becomes the world's first LEED-certified winery.

2006

Hawks & Hawks: **Château Boswell Winery.**

Bacchus Caves: **Waugh Cellars, Vin Roc/Fox Peak Vineyards, Dana Estates.**

Magorian Mine Services: **Keever Vineyards.**

Nordby Wine Caves: **Porter Family Vineyards.**

2008

Nordby Wine Caves: **Alexander Valley Vineyards, Rhys Vineyards.**

Hawks & Hawks: **Barnett Vineyards.**

Maldonado Family Vineyards built a wine cave.

California Wine Caves: The Napa Valley Reserve (fermentation room).

PRESENT

2005

Phase Two for Araujo Estate Wines by Alf Burtleson Construction.

Hawks & Hawks: **Kongsgaard.**

Anderthal Wine Caves: **Amphora Winery.**

Bacchus Caves: **Cliff Lede Vineyards, Bialla Vineyards.**

California Wine Caves: **Dierberg Estate Vineyards.**

Underground Associates: **Bravante Vineyards, Hundred Acre.**

Magorian Mine Services: **Arkenstone Vineyards, Freeman Winery, Boeschen Vineyards, Six Sigma Ranch & Vineyard, Lynmar Winery.**

Nordby Wine Caves: **Brown Estate, Blankiet Estate, Stone Tree Vineyard.**

2007

Magorian Mine Services: **Olney Family Vineyards.**

Nordby Wine Caves: **Kenzo Estate, Checkerboard Ranch.**

Hawks & Hawks: **Kelly Fleming Wines.**

Alf Burtleson Construction: **CADE Winery.**

The Cave Company: **Dutch Henry Winery.**

California Wine Caves: **Renteria Winery.**

Section 436 Winery Caves, which focuses on the use of subterranean space for winery facilities in natural or manmade caves, was added to the California Building Code.

2009

Since 1981 at least 150 wine caves and 50 private caves have been built in California.

Wine caves get national television exposure on *Dirty Jobs* with Mike Rowe.

Ferrari-Carano Vineyards & Winery

As dedicated, responsible stewards of many acres of vineyards in five appellations, Don and Rhonda Carano believed their wines deserved the ideal climatic aging conditions that caves can provide. Considering the vast acreage and the Caranos' desire to store three vintages at once, the cave complex would need to be large.

The Caranos visited countless caves throughout Napa Valley to get a feel for what would work best. Don shares, "After reviewing information with a team of geologists, engineers, Don Magorian and our winery operations team, we developed a system that we felt would meet our needs." The complex is configured as a grid with eight 390-foot tunnels bisected by four 436-foot tunnels. In some sections the crew managed 18 feet of progress a day, while in others where the conditions were more difficult, the progress slowed to two and a half feet per week. Soft rock formations such as shale and siltstone are between 2,500 and 5,000 psi. Medium rock—between 5,000 and 10,000 psi—includes sandstone, limestone and marble. Classified as hard are formations above 10,000 psi, including quartz, basalt and rhyolite. The hardest formations are found near the surface—where directional drilling operations are made—and rarely exceed 40,000 psi. According to Magorian, the mining conditions at Ferrari-Carano's cave were so difficult that he ran out of adjectives to describe how bad it could get. "We were continually working in highly fractured situations, encountering boulders the size of washing machines and a psi value of 14,000 within seams of soft, flaky clay. In a few places, we could look up into six- to 18-inch-wide cracks extending toward the surface."

Magorian's attention to detail, pacing and ability to keep the geometry perfect allowed challenges to be overcome and a beautiful space to come to fruition. When asked about this cave, Magorian's first words salute the Caranos' vision to purchase a rock crusher. One hundred percent of the cave spoils went through the rock crusher and were utilized throughout the vineyards in various ways: clay for the construction of reservoirs, rocks for drainage and roads, and in the vineyards small pebbles were incorporated into the soil. This was a natural step for Don and Rhonda, longtime leaders in sustainable-farming techniques. Drive Ferrari-Carano's vineyard ranches and you will swear the roads are paved like any other. They are paved, but not with the typical asphalt, gravel and concrete mixture. Lignin sulfonate—more commonly called tree sap, a byproduct of pulpwood processing—is used in combination with crushed rock. The tree sap-covered roads suppress dust, and because the material is biodegradable, no undesirable chemicals or compounds are washed into the vineyards and surrounding lands with rainfall.

Ferrari-Carano's sustainable practices extend far beyond its roads to include dry farming all hillside and mountain vineyards, integrating sheep and cows into and around vineyards, as well as attracting desirable birds and insects. In 2006 the California Land Stewardship Institute's Fish Friendly Farming Environmental Program certified Ferrari-Carano's Estate Vineyard in Dry Creek Valley.

The extensive cave system, holding more than 6,000 barrels of wine, fits perfectly with this sustainable approach—the entire complex is under a vineyard. Don Carano surmises: "Though harvest is where the critical decisions are made regarding the grapes' potential, it is only two out of 24 months of a red wine's life at a winery. Having a cave with invariant temperature and humidity allows us to maintain and better care for our barrels for the remaining 22 months. Our winemaking process, thankfully, does not include dealing with the difficulties inherent in warehouse barrel storage, thereby allowing us to focus our winemaking efforts in the vineyard and at the winery. During the heat of August or the chill of January, our Ferrari-Carano cave is a consistent 58 degrees."

Cave Size: 47,407 square feet
Cave Designers: Don and Rhonda Carano
Cave Contractor: Magorian Mine Services
Engineering Geologist and Tunneling Consultant: Scott Lewis, Condor Earth Technologies

Winery Specialties: Fumé Blanc, Chardonnay, Pinot Noir, Zinfandel, Merlot, Sangiovese, Cabernet Sauvignon

Montagna Napa Valley

The spectacular views from Montagna's estate encompass much of Napa Valley. The cave created for this winery spans the entire quarter-mile length of a hill along the edge of the Vaca Mountains adjacent to Chappellet's Pritchard Hill. Its south portal opens onto a garden of lawn, flowers and olive trees edged by balconies overlooking the valley floor a thousand feet below. For Bob Long, a businessman with the soul of an artist, the negative visual impact of a building on this picturesque sight was unthinkable. A cave was the right solution for both barrel storage and winemaking. The energy cost of cooling a storage facility on an exposed hilltop year-round versus going underground was also a contributing factor.

"The topography of 'Montagna' led us to the site very easily. We wanted to have an expansive landscaped area and needed a site for the future winery. We wanted to separate the back of the winery facility from the vineyards and gardens but needed to find a way of connecting these uses. The economical logic told us to connect Point A, the winery, to Point B, the South Portal Gardens, with a straight line. We opted for a design that took a little longer, approximately 1,512 in linear feet, to get from one point to the other, but the route would be much more interesting."

Early in the construction there was a slight cave in. After the repair, a rather large "concaved" portion of the ceiling was missing. Given the scope of the project, Bob concluded that they were not going to be concerned about finishing the cave with pure symmetry and perfect arches, and embraced the organic nature of the design with its deviations.

"In a project this size, we experienced mid-course corrections on a daily basis. Except for a few cave-ins and having the county require us to return to the cave after completion to provide another emergency exit from the middle of the mountain, the project ran very smoothly. The spoils from the cave were a great byproduct also, providing us excellent road base material for the property."

The cave complex is designed to serve two distinct functions: one, winemaking and barrel storage; the other, entertaining guests. For the latter, the south portal has a system installed below the cave floor that allows for heating, cooling and dehumidifying rooms created for dining, full kitchen and related storage.

According to winemaker Nile Zacherle, the caves offer a stable and consistent environment of temperature and humidity that make it possible to age the wine longer in the barrel without drying out fruit flavors and tannin. "The grapes come from the vineyards adjacent to the winery and cave area, allowing us a higher level of control when deciding what and how to pick at harvest time. The wine is racked far less frequently because of this more humid cave environment."

Cave Size: 20,692 square feet
Cave Designers: Lail Design Group; Robert W. Long; Underground Associates
Cave Contractor: Underground Associates

Winery Specialties: Cabernet Sauvignon, Cabernet Franc, Petit Verdot, Malbec, Syrah

Volumes of light cascade crosswise over hundreds of feet of a gently curved hillside cave. Standing in the main section of O'Shaughnessy Estate Winery's cave, one can easily feel diminutive. Located on a steep, remote area near the crest of Howell Mountain, O'Shaughnessy's cave exemplifies form following function—and its function is to age small quantities of cabernet sauvignon.

After the winery's first plantings in 1997, owner Betty O'Shaughnessy and winemaker Sean Capiaux soon decided that a cave would meet their needs. She did not want anyone to feel claustrophobic and wanted the best possible conditions for her wines and winemaker. They determined that a single level of barrels would be ideal. To accommodate four rows of barrels and pathways for equipment, a span of 26 feet was needed at the base, requiring a height of 20-22 feet at the top of the arch to create the correct forces to provide structural strength.

The suggestion by Vince Georges, the project engineer for Underground Associates at the time, of an infinity arc—an arc that appears to go on forever—appealed to Betty's aesthetic and sense of drama. With Betty's choice of color and lighting, the cave came together in a luminous, powerful way. The cave complex consists of a massive room some 370 feet in length curving gracefully 60-70 feet under the hillside that can access the outside by three separate tunnels each 90 feet long.

Winemaker Sean Capiaux was an integral part of the design team from the beginning, planning the vineyards and designing and outfitting the production side of the winery. His research showed that having hot, cold and ozone water hard-plumbed into the cave would make the cave function well. Above niches that can be used for steaming are 12-inch vents extending 75 feet up to the surface. These can be used for night cooling, but Sean says they haven't really needed to do this; the cave stays consistently 58 degrees Fahrenheit with 78-80 percent humidity. Sean's practice of doing no primary fermentation in the cave and not using fans to exchange air, as well as using only electric forklifts, reduces the chance of

introducing heat or altering humidity. A design factor of this cave also contributes to the constant conditions: The 90-foot entrance tunnels descend into the main room at a two-percent grade; thus the center of this cave is like a basin where the cooler air settles.

Uniquely, the cave has poured-in-place concrete rails under the barrels. Between the rails, the cement was formed into troughs with drains every 10 feet so that each barrel could be washed and rotated in place. For Brady Mitchell, whose company did the concrete work, creating those curved rails and keeping everything the exact distance was one of his most challenging jobs. One winter day he and his men were so engrossed in their work that when they came out they discovered it had snowed. With snow and the road out so steep, they ended up spending the night in the cave to stay warm.

While the majority of the 9,000 cubic yards of spoils were used to construct the pad on which the winery and office would sit, the remainder was used to construct roadways on the property. A small portion was incorporated under the soil in an undeveloped section of vineyard as an experiment for future planting.

In 2008, always planning for new eras in the business, Betty and her husband Paul Woolls converted one of the portal tunnels into a 13,000-bottle wine library and small dining area. The library and dining area are separated from each other and the cave by half-inch-thick glass walls and doors for insulation. As for Sean Capiaux, the quiet stillness and constant conditions in the cave are ideal for making wine. Not that the occasional Led Zeppelin song or the rolling thunder of his skateboard doesn't test the cave's wonderful acoustics.

Cave Size: 11,000 square feet
Cave Designers: Betty O'Shaughnessy; Sean Capiaux; Underground Associates
Cave Contractor: Underground Associates
Engineering Geologist and Tunneling Consultant: Scott Lewis, Condor Earth Technologies

Winery Specialty: Cabernet Sauvignon

Within the living rock of Napa's Mount George in a flawlessly engineered maze of tunnels and lofty domes, Palmaz Vineyards' winemaking and aging takes place. Four levels of interconnected tunnels penetrate the side of the mountain. The distance between the lowest tunnel and the top of the cave system's fermentation dome is equivalent to an 18-story building.

The fermentation dome—72 feet in diameter and 54 feet high—is one of the world's largest underground-reinforced structures. On a mezzanine within this dome, 24 stainless-steel fermentation tanks sit upon a custom carousel. The Palmaz crew handpicks the grapes and takes them to cool inside the cave's top level—Level 4. After de-stemming and a secondary handsorting, the grapes are conveyed to a crusher for gentle squeezing. With a click on the resident computer named Hal, the carousel turns, bringing the tank of choice underneath the crusher chute to receive the grapes and juice. Once fermentation is complete, pressing begins and the wine flows down to Level 3 and Level 2 to age in barrels.

The layout of these two levels is based on a wagon-wheel design. Once aged, the wine gently flows to the final level, where all of the bottling and packaging takes place. Through crushing, fermentation, barrel aging, blending and bottling, nothing but gravity moves the product—a key aspect of Palmaz Vineyards' winemaking.

During the nine years of building, an army of construction workers could be seen steadily crafting this underground creation, and Graham Wozencroft, the engineer guiding the project, seemed to live in the Underground Associates construction trailer when he wasn't roaming the vast complex growing into the hillside. The winery has exterior entrances at each level but is also vertically connected by a 150-foot-high shaft housing the stairs, tank elevator, passenger elevator and a duct for all the utilities. An innovative water-treatment facility, recycling 100 percent of the water use, is located within the lowest level.

This unique, collaborative project was a dream come true. The dream began soon after Julio Palmaz became a resident at the School of Medicine at the University of California, Davis. Amalia Palmaz shares: "At that time our friends were doctors or trying to be doctors and many were also kind of dancing around the idea of doing something with wine. We used to drive around the valley and dream. Many times driving around I would say 'Oh, why did I marry a doctor? I should have married a farmer.' I always felt that vineyard farming was just fascinating. And Julio would say, 'Well you're stuck with me and on top of that we'll never be able to afford this!' All too soon we needed to move to Texas for him to be able to do the research he needed. It was really hard but he kept saying that someday we would come back." Over the next several years, Julio made a host of discoveries and by 1983 had invented the world's first expandable coronary stent. Today, more than two million stents that derive from Dr. Palmaz's invention are placed in patients annually.

Amalia relates that in 1996, she said, "'Julio, do you remember that we said we would go back to California? Why not have a vineyard and a winery?' He said that I was out of my mind! The next day we were on the plane flying to California and came to the valley to see what was available. We love old places, and this old property with a history is what we found."

One of the first people they met was Dick Steltzner, who had a wine cave. Dick dreams big and suggested a "very ambitious project" for a gravity-flow winery. This layered cave idea stewed for two years while Underground Associates and Glen Ragsdale worked through their long waiting list. Finally, their schedules opened up and the multistory, underground building went into construction.

According to Amalia, "Actually, no one can take 100 percent of the credit for this project, and that is the beauty of it. We were really strangers absorbing everything that everyone was saying. Dick certainly had a lot to do with the basic concept of how to

implement gravity flow. John Lail had a lot to do with trying to conceptualize what we wanted to do. Everyone had something to do, and Graham seemed to solve every problem. I am to blame for the elevator concept since I refuse to climb so many stairs." Julio succinctly states, "We stand on the shoulders of everyone who built caves before us." The entire infrastructure is underground, keeping modern elements of the winery concealed and protecting the historic and aesthetic qualities of the property. The Palmazes are passionate about maintaining the property and the vineyards for generations to come.

Daughter Florencia concludes, "This is truly a family affair. It was my parents' dream to have their whole family together. The winery has made that dream a reality. With this special place we have all come together with a common passion for wine and honoring the land that is both our home and our livelihood. Today my father and mother live in the historic home of the estate, and my brother and I are nearby raising our families on the same land. After years of building and lots of digging, the winery is proud of making wine with supple texture that can be enjoyed in its youth while still exhibiting the structure and integrity of a wine that will last with cellaring."

Cave Size: 85,000 square feet
Cave Designers: Graham Wozencroft; Lail Design Group, Jon Lail, Howard Heid, Doug Osborn
Cave Contractor: Glen Ragsdale, Underground Associates
Structural Engineer: Jacobs Associates
Cave Finish and Floors Contractor: Brady Mitchell Construction

Winery Specialties: Cabernet Sauvignon, Chardonnay, Muscat Canelli, Johannisburg Riesling

When Stuart Sloan first planted grapes in 1997, his mission was to produce the highest quality fruit he could from this estate vineyard. He felt if he were fortunate enough to do just that, then a nice wine was sure to follow.

Stuart is a firm believer in paying meticulous attention to every step of Sloan Estate's viticulture practices to coax the very best fruit from the vines. To honor that commitment, a state-of-the-art winery and aging facility were required; and a wine cave, stacked with French oak barrels, was part of the plan from the beginning.

In 2000 Dale Wondergem began mining the last cave complex in his long career with Alf Burtleson Construction. Stuart and Dale developed a great relationship, refining the design together as Dale mined.

For six months Dale mined out the 700-foot tunnel that runs approximately 500 feet straight as a laser from the mouth of the vineyard; it shoots under the gardens, tennis court and driveway until it finally curves and connects to the back side of the winery, right under Sloan's French château-style house. Because of the structural elements of the house, the cave could not be lined up with the winery doors; however, a narrow crescent-shaped tunnel, just wide enough for a forklift, was designed as a connecting pathway. The narrow route was challenging with two turns of uneven radius. Dale would have to negotiate through this tight spot with the roadheader. This tight negotiation of space soon became the basis of a friendly wager between the two men—a bull's-eye was even placed on the wall where the roadheader's bits were to break through.

Once mined out, the next phase of the project was gracing the cave with stone and brick. Stuart explains: "The house has an old, European quality, and we wanted to make sure that everything we do—the vineyards, the gardens, the winery, everything—blends that Old World sensibility with New World winemaking techniques."

Guided by Stuart's attention to details, the authenticity of the brick and stone was crucial. Sloan traveled to Vienna, Austria, considered the brick capital of the world. "During the late 1800s and early 1900s in the Austro-Hungarian Empire, almost everything was built out of brick. Going to Vienna to find these bricks seemed logical. So I did. At that time, and it may still be happening, whole areas were being torn down for new construction. These old building bricks were considered almost junk, certainly salvage."

Yet this salvage makes the whole place—because of the size of the brick, the patina, the sheer crudeness. New brick simply doesn't look like this. The bricks were all handmade during the late 1890s and early 1900s, and many even have personalized initials or logos from the local brickyards where they were fired. Getting those 60,000 bricks from Vienna to the top of a steep hillside in Napa Valley was another matter. As a low-value but high-weight item, the freight cost a lot more than the bricks themselves. A team of four experienced brick masons from Europe and a local support man took another six months to create the European aesthetic using these vintage bricks and local stones. Another six months went into lighting and control systems, as the cave is computer controlled to assist with cooling when needed.

Asked what he would change now, Stuart answers quickly: "Not a thing. It's worked exactly the way we wanted it to, functions really well, and of course, looks beautiful. I love that cave—really, it's one of my favorite things I've done and designed over the years."

Winemaker Martha McClellan, who has been with Sloan Estate since 2001, echoes his feelings: "The cave is indeed beautiful and a lovely place to make wine. Most of the actual winemaking takes place in the winery and side rooms of the cave where we wash the barrels and do all the clean up. The cave's purpose is to provide a tranquil, peace-filled atmosphere for the wine to rest and age for two or more years before it finally goes to bottle."

Within the cave, Sloan Estate has the ability to completely control the atmosphere, allowing the winemakers to guide the wine's aging while limiting any undesirable mold growth on barrels or walls. Controlling these aspects promotes their philosophy of strictly limiting use of artificial cleaning agents or harmful methods and maintaining a balanced, clean and harmonious aging and work environment for wine and workers alike.

In the end, Martha explains the cave's real power: "The beauty of the cave contributes to the soul of the wine, nurtured from vine, to tank, to barrel and ultimately to bottle."

Cave Size: 9,000 square feet
Cave Designers: Stuart Sloan; Dale Wondergem; Lail Design Group
Cave Contractor: Alf Burtleson Construction
Engineer Geologist and Tunneling Consultant: Scott Lewis,
Condor Earth Technologies

Situated just north of the city of St. Helena, Vineyard 29 is one of the most technologically advanced wineries in Napa Valley. It's just what one might expect given that owner Chuck McMinn is a Silicon Valley high-tech industry veteran with razor-sharp intellect and a passion for technology and wine.

The construction team began boring in 2001, tunneling some 13,000 square feet beneath the surface. Lail Design Group's plan called for three distinct tunnels. The north and south tunnels converge at Vineyard 29's events room, a point reaching 125 feet back into the Mayacamas Mountains. Another 25 feet further into the mountainside lies the wine library, 75 feet directly beneath the sauvignon blanc vineyard behind the facility.

This particular tunnel configuration, a giant arch with one main artery, allows individual portions of the tunnel system to be designated for custom-crush use. Thus, each tunnel section serves as its own distinct cave space, allowing custom-crush clients the flexibility to treat their wines as they wish, and allowing Vineyard 29 to carry on the labor-intensive processes it employs in carefully aging each barrel.

Chuck wanted the caves to exude the same elegance as the winery's wine, uplifting the spirits of his staff and guests. The graceful arches and curves that appealed to his aesthetic are coated with a specially mixed shotcrete—a blend of white cement and white sand. But an unusual feature of this cave is the absence of light switches. Sensor-detected movement from tunnel to tunnel signals the overhead lights and music to magically turn on as one enters each room. And that's just the beginning of the winery's green features.

Tucked away in the north tunnel, air condensers allow for clean-air recycling, a constant 65 percent humidity and temperature maintenance, drawing cool air from the sauvignon blanc vineyard above down into the caves at night. The winery design is nearly 100 percent gravity fed to increase the quality of the wine produced and to substantially reduce the noise created by pumps and winemaking machinery. Special Capstone MicroTurbines generate all the winery's electricity on site and, in the process, derive all the hot and cold water for use in the facility as a byproduct. The system produces about a tenth of typical utility power emissions. Overall the winery is over 250 percent more efficient in natural-resource use than a typical grid-power winery. Additionally, Vineyard 29 has its own underground wells and septic system so that all the water used is sourced, used and treated on site: The environmental impact is about as minimal as a facility's can be.

"Too many factors can adversely affect a wine during the aging process—the wines' formative years, so to speak," Chuck relates. He and his team ensure that these years are pure benefit to the wine; Vineyard 29 takes extreme care to keep the caves in optimal condition, both in terms of temperature regulation and in overall cleanliness—any exposure to unwanted elements might be harmful to aroma and flavor.

With technology and sustainability every bit as important as aesthetic value, the winery and its wines score high marks on all accounts.

Cave Size: 13,000 square feet
Cave Designers: Chuck McMinn; Lail Design Group, Jon Lail, Doug Osborn, Howard Heid; Don Magorian
Cave Contractor: Magorian Mine Services
Engineering Geologist and Tunneling Consultant: Scott Lewis, Condor Earth Technologies

Winery Specialties: Vineyard 29 Cabernet Sauvignon, Vineyard 29 Sauvignon Blanc, Vineyard 29 Cabernet Franc, Vineyard 29 Aida Cabernet Sauvignon, Vineyard 29 Aida Zinfadel, Vineyard 29 Cru

Left: Before cave construction began, a small hole was bored into the hillside. The location could not have been more perfect. As part of the gravity-flow process, wine is lifted in the elevator and transferred through that small hole down to the wine cave, where it is placed in French oak barrels for aging. Because the winery produces its own electricity, the cost for this convenience is negligible.

Above and Right: The air vent on the hillside vineyard is 75 feet directly above the library, tucked in the farthest reach of the cave.

Throughout 2001 drivers cruising up and down the Silverado Trail most likely glanced to the hills on the west side of the highway as they passed by. Four large, gaping black holes had appeared and were spread out evenly across the base. Months later the round black holes began to disappear, first behind growing mounds of earth coming out and then behind the construction of a state-of-the-art building with the latest winemaking technology.

Agustin and Valeria Huneeus had purchased the property a decade earlier and christened it Quintessa—a name alluding to the five dramatic hills and five distinct microclimates included in the property's diverse geography, and which tied to their belief that the property was destined to be a quintessential wine estate. Their combined passion and intensity required a winery facility that would fulfill all their needs while creating minimal disruption to the natural elements of the land.

Agustin's goal was to produce a single wine expressing the best creation of the vineyard's Bordeaux varieties each year. Like most classic wines, the label would name the vineyard, not the varietals.

Valeria Huneeus, who holds a Ph.D. in microbiology, is a viticulturist and a passionate steward of the land. From the beginning, she directed Quintessa's farming with sustainable practices that sought harmony with the soil, vegetation and animal life. Since 2004 the entire 170-acre vineyard property has been farmed under strict Biodynamic principles.

The Huneeuses chose Walker Warner Architects of San Francisco to design their winery and caves to blend into the contours of the property. The graceful crescent-shaped structure was carefully considered for its environmental sensitivity. It fits snugly into an eastern-facing hillside, disrupting little of the natural beauty of the property. A façade of stone and landscaping of native plants and oaks creates a striking presence amid the diverse terrain.

Hidden now along the back wall of the winery, those four large portals lead into almost a quarter mile of graceful functional tunnels designed for 3,000 French oak barrels. There, wine made from each block in the vineyard is aged for up to two years before the components are brought together and the final Quintessa blend is created. The wine is then bottled and laid down for yet another year before release.

A second small cave was created on the hillside above the large, lower barrel-aging complex. Its portal forms the back wall of the finished reception and tasting rooms located in the center of the winery office building. The little cave, called the Enoteca, is used for tastings.

Quintessa wine bears the same name as the vineyard from which it is made—in broad terms, Quintessa is a red Meritage wine.

Cave Size: 17,000 square feet
Cave and Winery Designer: Walker Warner Architects
Cave Contractor: Underground Associates

Winery Specialty: Meritage

Bella Vineyards

In an out-of-the-way corner of rural Sonoma County, visitors are offered a tasting in the charming Bella cave, treated like family by a very friendly and approachable staff.

Scott and Lynn Adams chose to have a cave built for many reasons. First and foremost were the conditions the cave would afford for aging their high-quality, small-production zinfandel and syrah varietal wines from Sonoma County vineyards. Second was the ability to increase barrel-storage capacity without removing vines, which would have been required for an aboveground facility. Additionally, their Bella property offered an ideal, north-facing hillside for cave construction.

Another reason, Scott enthusiastically shares, "is the long-term energy savings and environmental friendliness of aging wine in a cave; we used zero electricity for cooling in the middle of a 105 degree July heat wave in Dry Creek Valley."

Excavation began in June 2002 and was quite an experience for the Adams family. Scott good-naturedly relates, "Baseball-sized rocks descended on the crush pad like a meteor shower with that first blast of dynamite during construction. I took a shrapnel hit in the shoulder during the first blast, but lived to tell about it. We were sure to distribute baskets filled with earplugs, Excedrin, flowers and plenty of Bella wine to all of our neighbors to help ease the pain of noise and dust."

Finally completed in December of 2003, the caves accommodate barrel storage and working space as well as entertainment space.

Scott, Lynn and winemaker Joe Healy knew they wanted a good flow and access, so a horseshoe-shaped main corridor was adopted. To add storage and working space in the production side of the cave, four barrel rooms, one alcove for a racking tank, and one utility/storage room were all added. For visual interest and retail space, the public/tasting side of the cave features one room and several alcoves.

"We can now perform all of our post-fermentation winemaking practices in the safety and comfort of a temperature-controlled environment. This allows us to time racking and topping of barrels on the schedule appropriate for the wine and not the seasonal climate. Also maturation is slow and paced, allowing for extended barrel aging and oak integration," Joe explains.

Visitors can taste wine in the caves and see the inner workings of the winery. The entertainment area is complete with a beautiful dining room, tasting area and music room. It is the site for many fun, winery-related events such as winemaker dinners, special reserve tastings, cooking classes and a variety of musical performances.

Cave Size: 7,000 square feet
Cave Designers: Scott and Lynn Adams; Joe Healy; Dave Provost
Cave Contractor: Bacchus Caves

Winery Specialties: Zinfandel, Syrah

Jericho Canyon Vineyard

Jericho Canyon Vineyard is not just a vineyard or a winery or a cave. It is a complex of interlocking parts that work in harmony with one another. Each complements the next. Certified as a fish-friendly, sustainable farm, Jericho Canyon Vineyard has as little impact as possible on the environment.

Dale and Marla Bleecher found this property in the 1980s and immediately knew it was the place they wanted to raise their three children. Originally given in a land grant to a veteran of the Civil War as payment for his services, the ranch is situated at the base of Mt. St. Helena along the road to the old Silverado Mine. The property had been used as a cattle ranch since the 1930s but showed evidence of a pre-Prohibition vineyard alongside Jericho Creek. The Bleechers replanted the old vineyard and extended it up the canyon, terracing extensively because of the steepness of the terrain.

Careful and exacting work that began in the vineyard is mirrored in the winery and in the cave. Dale recalls the inspiration: "We were interested in building a winery with minimal impact on our surroundings. By building wine caves, we were able to eliminate the use of energy for cooling, while at the same time avoiding the need to build a barrel warehouse, which we felt would take away from the natural setting."

The complex needed to fit comfortably in its surroundings, a canyon location. The winery building itself is designed like an old Napa Valley barn. The physical constraints of the topography—the hillsides and Jericho Creek—along with the existing buildings, dictated where the winery would be placed. The Bleechers' main interest was to build a simple, functional and efficient winery, and to give a sense of belonging. The simplicity and functionality of the cave reveal clean lines, elegant, cathedral-style intersections and a "window" to the world of volcanic tuft that encircles the cave—all evidence of the expert workmanship of Dale Wondergem, his son Ricky and the rest of the cave drilling team. While the original H-shape design was first suggested by Alf Burtleson, it was Dale Wondergem who ultimately influenced the design the most.

The drilling of the cave was not just a mechanical construction project for the Bleechers. As Marla explains, "Cave drilling is an art, with the artist being the manipulator of the machine. The driller must feel his way through, knowing when he has gone far enough; he must stop to shotcrete in order to protect his team from falling rock, knowing and understanding the rock so as to create the cleanest line, knowing his machines so they continue to work in an efficient and safe manner. It's dirty work to be sure, but it's exciting to see the caves take shape." Marla continues, "There were days when we would walk into the cave and the walls were sculptural. They looked like someone had come in and created forms that were trying to escape from the rock. The walls reminded me of Michelangelo's uncompleted sculptures, with figures struggling to release themselves from the volcanic tuft. I hated to have Ricky and Dale continue, as these forms soon turned to silent rock again. Because of the water and moisture behind our walls, we decided not to leave the rock face exposed; but Dale left us the window—the teeth of the mining tool are faint pictures to remind us of the cave's creation."

Though there was quite a bit of rain during the winter of the cave's construction, the dig went smoothly. However, a nearby spring, one that now helps to cool and maintain the humidity in the cave, caused an earlier start for the second tunnel. Once completed, the cave allowed Jericho Canyon to run its responsible practice throughout the property. And the same goes with its winemaking. Through gentle treatment and minimal intervention, the winery hopes to let the grapes speak for themselves as they are transformed from fruit to wine. Thus Jericho Canyon's small, intensely flavored grapes move from their rugged terraced hillside to the winery within their midst and finish in a peaceful, cool cave where they are allowed to evolve into a beautiful wine.

Cave Size: 6,000 square feet
Cave Designer and Contractor: Alf Burtleson Construction

Winery Specialties: Jericho Canyon Vineyard Cabernet Sauvignon, Jericho Canyon Vineyard Sauvignon Blanc

Boeschen Vineyards

Standing in the Boeschens' garden, one finds that the thought of a winery being near is vaporized by the sweet fragrance of flowers. Susan Boeschen's efforts of creating the feel of a garden that might have been planted at the time the house was built cast an enchanting spell.

When she first saw the house and property, she was taken by the vintage charm and the bones of an old garden. According to local lore, the house and barn were built circa-1880 by a prominent businessman for his mistress. The property was subsequently the retreat of a Russian princess—a prune and walnut orchard, a camellia nursery and a Christmas tree farm with each of the eras contributing to the collection of mature trees, including a vineyard planted by Hans Kornel.

"The property also had, higher up on the hill, a 275-foot, hand-dug, man-sized cave, which had been made about 100 years ago in a probable search for water." Dann Boeschen shares, "Knowing that the mountain was stable volcanic tuff we planned on a cave for barrel storage when we obtained our winery permit. When we decided to go forward with the winery, the lack of non-vineyard level land and aesthetic concerns about the look of our estate led us to put it all in the hill."

Functionally, the Boeschens had to accommodate fermentation, barrel storage, finished wine storage, office space and tasting rooms. Airflow for temperature and humidity control were considered, as well as the ease of access to the fermentation room from the outside crush pad. "We were going to handle the fruit gently—no must pumps and long hoses," recalls Dann. "Aesthetically, I was carrying in my mind a magazine article picture of a European wine cellar with a staircase and barrels on two levels. I also wanted to maximize the 'fun and interest' factor in the cave, however small it would be. After all, I was only going to get to dig in the ground once."

Dann brought aboard Don Magorian and Jon Lail to configure the cave. Don proposed an S-curve entry to provide an element of visual surprise in a small, relatively short cave, and bounced many other ideas back and forth as the excavation proceeded. Jon weighed the pros and cons of previous caves to find what would work here. Considering the options, Dann personally developed the serpentine upper exit and the unusual fermentation room.

The S-curve entrance provides an element of interest upon arrival at the fermentation room, giving a great view of the exposed rock wall in a cathedral-like setting. The two wall sections show the layers of volcanic sediment, while the observation and tasting mezzanine features a hand-dug, serpentine exit into the garden above. The compacted volcanic ash was very consistent, just as in the century-old cave higher on the hill. It was a true cave digger's dream: Cut as long as you want with no faults, soft spots or cave-ins, then add the shotcrete when it is convenient.

With the cave's natural temperature in the low 60s, very little effort is needed to guide the wine's development. Because so little heating and cooling energy are required for the cave, Boeschen is able to generate all the electricity needed to run the winery with the solar panels that were installed.

This burying of the winery has not only streamlined the winemaking process, but its invisibility complements the dedication to the care of vineyards and grounds. A grand White Lady Banks Rose estimated to be more than 120 years old reigns there. Her branches that devoured an arbor and reach far into the trees cover a remarkable winemaking operation beneath the surface.

Cave Size: 5,500 square feet
Cave Designers: Lail Design Group, Jon Lail, Rick Baker;
Don Magorian; Boeschen Family
Cave Contractor: Magorian Mine Services
Engineering Geologist and Tunneling Consultant: Scott Lewis,
Condor Earth Technologies
Concrete Contractor: Brady Mitchell

Winery Specialties: Cabernet Sauvignon, Bordeaux-style blends

Château Boswell Winery

"The rabbit-hole went straight on like a tunnel for some way, and then dipped suddenly down...she had plenty of time as she went down to look about her and to wonder what was going to happen next..." —Lewis Carroll's *Alice's Adventures in Wonderland*.

"Like Alice in Wonderland, each day was another adventure for me," says Susan Boswell, an avid rock collector since childhood. While Château Boswell Winery's cave was being created, Susan kept a pile of geology books, including *The Winemaker's Dance*, on her nightstand for reference about the excavation happenings of the day. "I wanted the cave entrance to be barely visible; Stephen Hawks likened my portal to a rabbit hole in the side of our steep hillside vineyard."

At the base of Glass Mountain, the crew excavated 65 feet below the earth's surface, unfolding 4 million years of volcanic geological history before their eyes. According to geologists Jonathan Swinchatt and David Howell, the bright orange rubbly rock possibly represents a soil zone baked by the heat of the volcanic ash as it accumulated on the surface. Most of these intriguing patterns of stone remain exposed, lending another natural dimension to Château Boswell's desire to leave as little imprint upon this virgin land as possible. The process of excavating the cave brought Susan closer to the earth's history, creating an even more dedicated approach to the importance that the preservation of land, water and air has to the future of Napa Valley. "We continue to strive to be responsible to our community's ongoing dependence upon a strong environmental structure by being a sustainable winery and an agricultural property," relates Susan. Château Boswell became the first certified Napa Green Winery in 2007. "Our vineyards and landscaping are all maintained organically by hand labor, ours and our employees, and with this closeness to our land and fruit we have developed a very sensitive and attentive approach to the production of our handcrafted wines."

Château Boswell's vast cave was constructed to green-building specifications with special attention to long-term energy and water conservation. The result was a doubling of facility space without any increase in energy usage thanks to a new ventilation system that rendered the existing HVAC system unnecessary. The ventilation system design was a modern play on an old idea of using piping under the ground to cool the air flowing in. Beneath the cave floor, a 24-inch-diameter duct runs from an outside fresh-air supply fan for a run of 300-plus feet. An exhaust fan in the tank room pulls the fresh air through the entire cave and tank room, keeping a year-round temperature of 55 to 58 degrees and a perfect humidity level.

The topography of the property and the winery's goal to incorporate the cave into the existing facility led to the split-level design. The primary entrance is located at the base of the estate vineyard and opens into a domed wine library. Obsidian fragments, plentiful in the vineyard soils, have been incorporated into the floor. Glass doors guard the stairs, which lead down to the intersection of the main barrel hall. In addition to the 410-foot-long main barrel hall, seven 24- to 48-foot-long alcoves were added for barrel storage or extra fermentation space. With a width of 15 feet and an average ceiling height of 16 feet, Château Boswell has achieved a desired balance of form and function.

"At Château Boswell, we remain committed to our philosophy of zero-compromise winemaking and small-lot premium wines that display the unique characteristics of our vineyard sources through Old World low-intervention winemaking techniques. Whether it is berry-by-berry sorting for our cabernet or the gentle stirring of our barrel-fermented chardonnay, winemaker Luc Morlet has clearly displayed his talents and his belief in a quality-without-compromise approach."

Cave Size: 11,000 square feet
Cave Designers: Susan Boswell; R. Thornton Boswell; Joshua Peeples
Cave Contractor: Hawks & Hawks Wine Caves
Cave Excavators: Dale and Ricky Wondergem
Artistic Consultant: Michael Johnson

Wines produced at Chateau Boswell under Luc Morlet's direction include Chateau Boswell Wines, Jacquelynn Wines, Bure Family Wines, Carte Blanche Wine and Morlet Family Vineyards

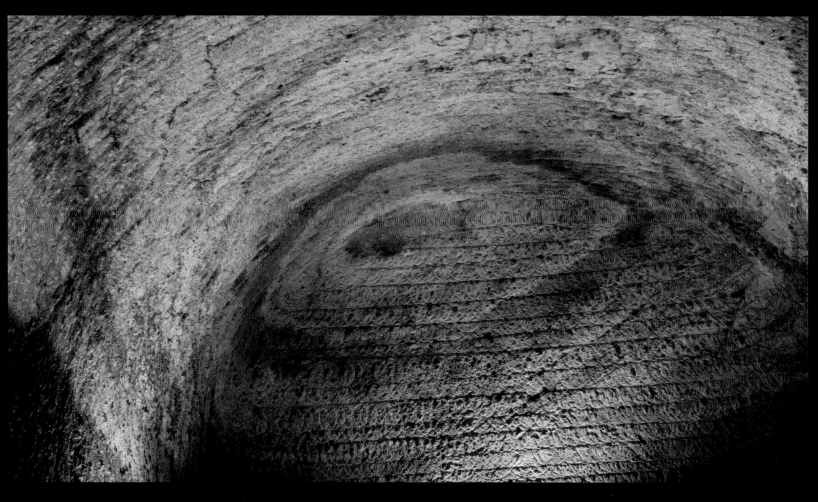

For years the old stone walls of the ghost winery built by H W Helms in the 1880s stood quietly tucked against a hillside at the base of the Mayacamas Mountains just south of St. Helena. An idyllic place of crumbling stones and vines, it seemed almost a natural outcropping of rocks emerging from the hill. Photographing there years ago, I stood amid the few standing walls and looked down the steps into a roofless room and then through the arched window of a freestanding wall and could almost hear whispers of forgotten voices. A rich sense of history persisted and lingers still. From these ruins, magnificence has emerged.

In 2005 Mr. Hi Sang Lee was drawn to the story of this old relic when he acquired the property from Livingston Moffett Winery. Protecting and honoring the integrity of the historic ruins was paramount in his goal of creating a world-class winery of the highest standard. He chose Howard Backen and John Taft of Backen Gillam Architects to help guide his vision for a new winery at the site. These men worked closely with winemaker Philippe Melka and production manager Cameron Vawter to develop the caves' configuration, function and scale. A small loop cave had been built behind the ruins for barrel storage. The new winery was designed to hide within and behind the ruins, with the bulk of the facilities being placed within a greatly expanded cave system. The caves now handle a portion of all facets of the winemaking, from fermentation to hospitality, from barrel aging and bottling to case-goods storage.

While the initial goal was to produce one vineyard-designate wine, the project expanded toward three world-class vineyard-designate wines from three distinct elevations and soil types in Napa. Mr. Lee insisted that organic farming be a part of the plan and brought in Cameron Vawter to collaborate. Cameron explains, "The Helms Vineyard was farmed organically from the purchase in 2005; we became CCOF certified in 2008. The Hershey and Lotus vineyards are also farmed organically and will be certified in 2010. The farming philosophy is one of complete sustainability and I hope someday we will have a complete circle with few outside inputs. We have incorporated animals for weed control and bees for pollination."

The team designed the winery and caves with these three vineyards in mind. Three fermentation rooms—one for each vineyard—provide ideal conditions. The barrel fermentation room can be heated to the mid-80s and then cooled to the 50s, if necessary. The cave houses five different temperature zones that can be individually controlled. Humidity and airflow are key to maintaining the oak tanks, and the separate oak-tank fermentation room allows them to be maintained with little input. Custom-fashioned doors facilitate fresh airflow. State-of-the-art concrete tanks are housed in the fermentation barn, providing a third option for the winemaking team.

The cave has enough space to age barrels for 24 months or longer without stacking and includes room for a bottling line and bottle storage for the years prior to release. The luxury of space allows the wine to be worked as gently as possible and gives the winemaker 100 percent control from crushing to bottle aging.

During excavation of one of the larger barrel-aging cellars, the soil condition was discovered to be poor, so a decision was made to just continue the cave with a standard narrow profile until better soil conditions were found. The cave was mined for an additional 100 feet at a 14-foot width before the soil conditions improved to allow the cave to expand out to the desired 26-foot-wide cellar.

Howard explains, "One of the great benefits of a cave is that, unlike with buildings, you have flexibility to change the layout as tunnels are being built since the spaces can only be perceived from the interior, freeing up the design from the constraints of exterior influences that are created by a building."

When the last section of the cave was excavated, Mr. Lee and the key figures involved in the project held a hardhat champagne toast as the roadheader broke through the wall. Several hours after the celebration but before the walls and ceiling were structurally secured with wire mesh and shotcrete, a large boulder fell out of the ceiling right where the group had been standing for the toast and photos!

Over the course of three years the old stone structure was stabilized and reconstructed. Walking from the courtyard through the grand rotunda wine cellar and into the cave is a pivotal experience for visitors and the winemaking team. The rotunda creates the transition between the historic stone winery and the new winemaking facilities as well as a buffer between temperature zones. The materials, shape and light of the magnificent wine cellar perfectly integrate the courtyard's open outdoor environment with the dark, quieter spaces within the caves.

Cave Size: 20,000 square feet
Cave Designers: Mr. Hi Sang Lee; Howard Backen; John Taft; Philippe Melka; Cameron Vawter
Cave Contractor: Bacchus Caves
General Contractor: Ledcor Construction

Winery Specialty: Cabernet Sauvignon

Keever Vineyards

The hillsides west of Yountville rise quickly and steeply up from the valley floor. In 1999 Bill and Olga Keever discovered a horse ranch, complete with barns, corrals and a riding arena. They fell in love with the site and its panoramic views of the Yountville appellation. However, they had dreamed of a vineyard, not a horse ranch. The first thing they did—even before rebuilding the house—was plant vines.

Developing the property was a major undertaking. "We were severely restricted as to how many acres of our property we could plant because of the sloping hills that make up much of it," recalls Bill. "The first acre and a half that we planted soon after purchasing the property was the horse corrals and riding arena, because flat surfaces had been cut into the hillsides long ago when such undertakings were not regulated or monitored. It is a different story today, and ultimately we were allowed to plant another three and a half acres." Over the course of seven years, the property was transformed. Some hillsides were intentionally left unplanted, reserved for indigenous wildlife. Owl boxes and a raptor perch were added to keep pest species in check while remaining environmentally neutral.

The site now includes a winery and tasting room and, of course, caves. Bill had some ideas early on: "From the minute we decided to move beyond being a grower and actually make wine—possibly at our own facility—we knew we wanted a cave for barrel aging.

After using the available flat ground for some of our vineyard blocks and for the winery site, there wasn't enough flat ground left to build another building. Plus the benefits of going into the hill outweighed any other option."

Selecting the best hillside was key because the cave needed close proximity to the winery. Tunnel consultant Scott Lewis provided the basic design. Don Magorian was responsible for the artistry, special features and excavation. The very wet winter of 2005-2006, which was marked by Highway 29 flooding on New Year's Eve, delayed completion of the cave by six months.

The cave and winery were both completed in the early summer of 2006. This small family winery is operated by Bill and Olga and their two children, Ashley and Jason, all under the direction of winemaker Celia Welch.

Cave Size: 3,250 square feet
Cave Designer: Scott Lewis
Cave Contractor: Magorian Mine Services
Engineering Geologist and Tunneling Consultant: Scott Lewis, Condor Earth Technologies

Winery Specialties: Cabernet Sauvignon, Sauvignon Blanc

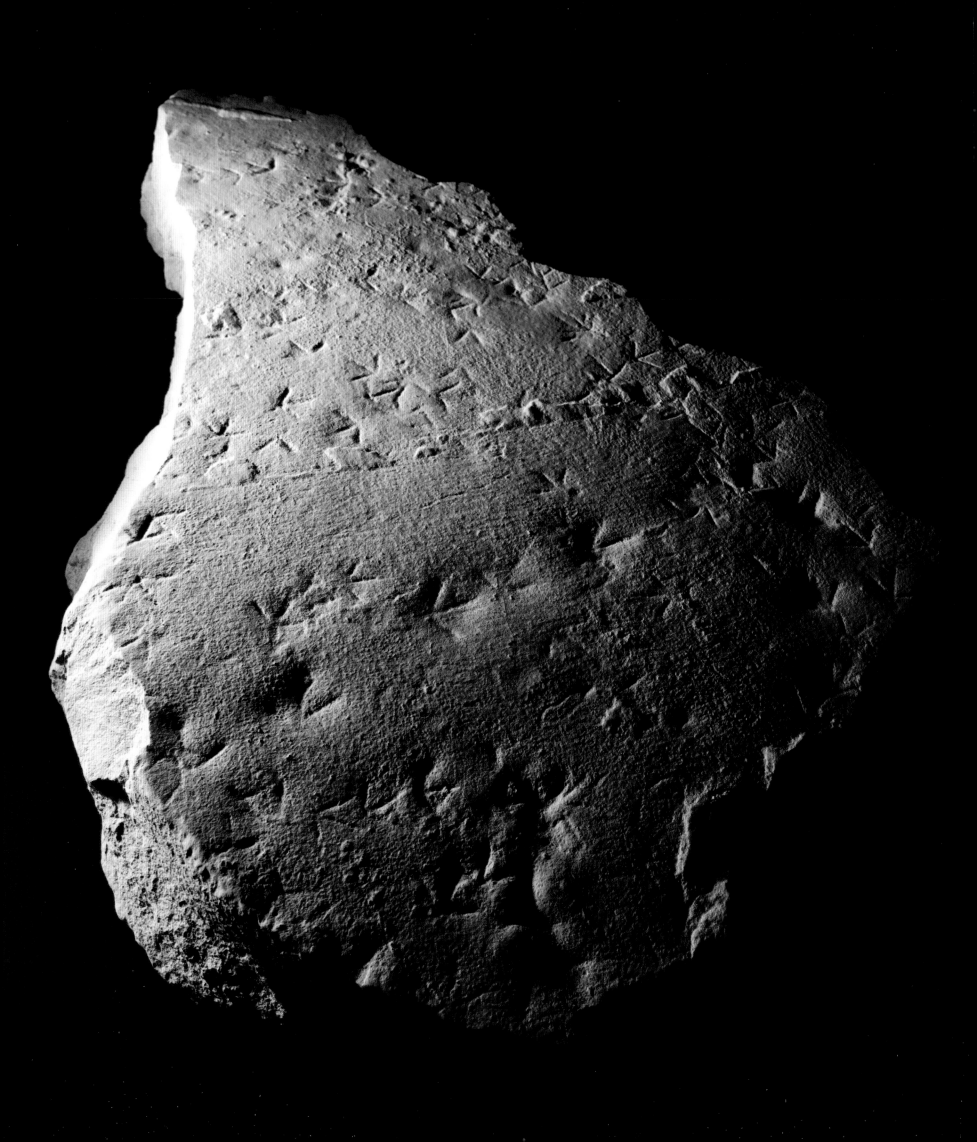

Porter Family Vineyards

At the time the Porter family made the decision to create a cave, they had no idea that this adventure into the earth would provide more than one story to savor. This scientifically minded family saw the benefits of placing their winery in a cave as compelling. Being energy efficient, preserving the vines and hiding the winery from view in the charming rolling hills of the southern end of Napa, known as Coombsville, made the decision simple.

The 500-foot cave tunnel penetrates through a steep terraced hill of vineyard from east to west in a lazy-S configuration with side tunnels for fermentation, blending, barrel wash, laboratory work and storage. The soil conditions, pure layered sandstone, were some of the finest Nordby Wine Caves had experienced, and construction went as planned without major obstacles. Most cave projects encounter something unexpected as miners tunnel their way through the earth—a seam of water or sand or extremely hard rock that necessitates improvising, changing direction, among other issues. Although no major obstacles were discovered during this dig, something truly unique was encountered halfway through the cave boring at Porter Family Vineyards.

The ceiling of the gently curving tunnel bore was approximately 40 feet deep into the earth under the crest of the hill. One evening, in the silent darkness, a large flat chunk of sandstone dropped from the ceiling. The next morning immediate excitement spread through the cave when sandpiper footprints were discovered, imprinted on the top of the stone!

Tom Porter relates, "Our daughter Heather, our 'in-house biologist,' contacted a paleontologist at UC Berkeley who estimated the prints to be between 5 and 20 million years old. At one time these beautiful hills must have been a beach or shoreline of an ancient lake! The sandstone with fossilized prints has since become our winery's trademark."

What a blending of ancient and new this wine cave represents, as precise computer control of cave conditions, with minimum energy usage through night air cooling and optimum control of ventilation, is monitored and regulated by sensors placed throughout the cave. In the event of dangerous levels of carbon dioxide being detected, four large variable-speed ventilation fans would be brought to full speed, replacing 100 percent of the air in less than 10 minutes.

A unique aspect of this cave is found in the large blending bayside tunnel. It has one wall that is straight and vertical—instead of the classic arch—and was engineered to enable the efficient utilization of space for the large vertical blending tanks. Gentle gravity-flow processing of the grapes ensures that the fruit yields wines of world-class quality. All fermentation is completed in small-lot two-ton stainless tanks that are temperature controlled during fermentation to give measurable, predictable and repeatable results.

The cave tailings were placed in a natural ravine at the west cave portal, precluding the need to haul them to another site for disposal. In addition, these compacted spoils created a nearly half-acre area that now supports the crush pad, cave mechanical and electrical support systems as well as the mobile bottling line.

Besides discovering fossilized bird prints the Porter family has another unique story attached to their cave. When the tunneling neared completion, the Discovery Channel program *Dirty Jobs* with Mike Rowe arrived to film an episode called "Cave Digger." Nordby Wine Caves allowed Mike to operate their roadheader for the last three or four feet, breaking through the other side of the hill and documenting this climactic event for many to see.

Cave Size: 17,000 square feet
Cave Designers: Tom Porter; Ken Bernards; Richard Perry; John Shook; Steven Wolfe; Neil Peoples
Cave Contractor: Nordby Wine Caves

Winery Specialties: Estate Cabernet Sauvignon, Estate Syrah

CADE Winery

The moment PlumpJack general manager John Conover saw the opportunity to purchase a special Howell Mountain vineyard property and create a winery, he also saw an opportunity and responsibility as a local resident to do it with the lightest of footprints. Fellow partners San Francisco Mayor Gavin Newsom and philanthropist Gordon Getty were quick to agree.

CADE Winery—named for a cask or barrel in Shakespeare's time—is one of the country's greenest construction projects, achieving LEED Gold certification. Below the winery, rocky hillside vineyards facing southwest at nearly 1,800 feet elevation are being farmed organically.

John shares, "We spent a lot of time interviewing a number of individuals before we chose Juan Carlos Fernandez of Lail Design Group. Though he had never designed a cave or a winery we felt he truly got what it was we wanted."

What CADE got was an environmentally conscious young architect who brought a mentality rooted in a unique design, where concrete, steel and glass were the chosen elements of construction rather than the traditional stone-and-wood vernacular of many Napa Valley wineries.

"CADE definitely gets its personality from the location," says Juan Carlos. "The first impression that we wanted to create for this project was one of visual excitement." Looking up to the top of the winery building he adds, "While the traditional barn has a pitched roof, CADE has an inverted roof that slants into the middle for water catchment that is stored for the vineyard."

Instead of quarrying stone and harvesting redwood for construction materials, Juan Carlos chose concrete with integral earth colors, steel made from 98-percent recycled material and hundreds of square feet of glass for a well-lit working environment that also uses less energy—even old blue jeans were used in the insulation.

Carved deep into the steep mountainside, right behind the winery, is a beautiful network of caves that provide a perfect 65-degree, high-humidity barrel-aging environment for the CADE cabernets. This is the first cave to have a ceiling that overlaps its walls, providing a hidden perch for light fixtures that softly illuminate the underground spaces. The dramatic curves and angles of the cave's multiple tunnels trace the shape of the PlumpJack shield, seen on that winery's labels—an element Juan Carlos has called "the ghost of PlumpJack." He adds, "Grape growing and winemaking is a process of discovery. The caves are about discovery, too. There are no straight lines, and around every curve you don't know what you'll see next."

Within the cave is a grand room that some feel is shaped similar to a snake that has just swallowed a large meal, as the dimensions are different throughout the space. The largest dimensions in the room range from a height of about 21 feet to a width of 38 feet. The height of the arches at the ends is 11 feet.

Geotechnical consultant Scott Lewis explains that the conditions for cave construction were as perfect as it gets. "Just pure uninterrupted volcanic tuff facilitated Alf Burtleson Construction in mining out the unique cave configuration. In any other conditions Juan Carlos's unique design may not have been so easy or even possible to do."

CADE winemaker Tony Biagi loves this new cave: "The variables of winemaking are enough to drive a winemaker mad. With caves, we are allowed to subtract one enormous variable, the huge fluctuation of temperatures of a barrel chai. Knowing that the wines are aging in a temperature range of no more than two or three degrees year-round allows my team and me to focus on the other infinite variables of winemaking to improve or maintain quality."

Cave Size: 15,000 square feet
Cave Designers: Lail Design Group; Juan Carlos Fernandez
Cave Contractor: Alf Burtleson Construction
Engineering Geologist and Tunneling Consultant: Scott Lewis, Condor Earth Technologies

Winery Specialties: CADE Estate Cabernet Sauvignon Howell Mountain, CADE Cabernet Sauvignon Howell Mountain, CADE Sauvignon Blanc Napa Valley, cade Napa Cuvée Cabernet Sauvignon

Dutch Henry Winery

"There is a Hobbit in all of us who loves to be underground," says Scott Chafen with a twinkle in his eyes when speaking of his family's decision to have a wine cave built.

Aside from that fundamental subterranean urge, the Chafen family is serious about their winemaking, energy use and farming practices. "First and foremost was the quality of wine. Caves just can't be beat for their consistency in temperature and humidity. We had already installed solar panels, and a cave was yet another way to save energy and reduce our carbon footprint while providing a year-round covered and temperature-controlled working environment."

The family worked closely with Vincent Georges, owner of The Cave Company, in designing and creating their cave. Functionality from a winemaking standpoint was critical, as was the creation of a larger room dedicated for tastings and small gatherings. The exterior was designed to have minimal impact on the surrounding environment. As a certified-organic farm, Dutch Henry Winery even planted olive trees on the hillside of the main portal.

Though relatively new, the cave looks as if it has always been there. The stonework on both portals was sourced from the winery's vineyard in St. Helena, and a local mason did the rockwork.

Scott has been at the helm of every vintage since the family winery began in 1992. He describes himself as a "winemaker, cellar rat, sales guy, office manager, landscaper, olive picker, architect, delivery boy, forklift extraordinaire, customer service rep…ah, the myriad opportunities in family business." One of those opportunities got exciting when he had the privilege of working with The Cave Company: "I was able to say, 'Fire in the hole,' and ignite 750 pounds of dynamite!"

According to Vincent, who supervised that detonation very closely, "About 60 linear feet of the cave—about 20 percent—was in very old and hard volcanic rock typical of the foothills of Calistoga. That forced us to use dynamite and re-determine the location of the entertainment room."

Once layers of shotcrete are applied, there is no way to know if the walls were created with a roadheader or drill and blasting. Wanting to add an instructive feature for their guests, the Chafen family had Vince create two identical "windows" through the shotcrete to the bare rock: One is located where blasting occurred, and the other reveals the picking marks of the roadheader.

The Chafens are very pleased with their cave, and Scott and his crew are a happy group who obviously love what they do. They enjoy having this special place in the hill to craft their wine and share it with visitors.

Cave Size: 4,500 square feet
Cave Designers: Chafen Family; Vincent Georges
Cave Contractor: The Cave Company

Winery Specialties: Los Carneros Chardonnay, Napa Valley Rosé, Napa Valley Pinot Noir, Napa Valley Argos (Bordeaux-style blend), Napa Valley Estate Cabernet Sauvignon, Napa Valley Cabernet Franc, Napa Valley Merlot, Napa Valley Reserve Cabernet Sauvignon, Napa Valley Estate Syrah, Napa Valley "Terrier Station" Cabernet, Napa Valley Zinfandel

Building a safe and legal wine cave requires determining and obtaining necessary building codes and permits—California varies by county. After that, all you need is a good working knowledge of mining machines and a keen awareness of the site's geology—and perhaps a license to explode dynamite. Most of us, of course, do not fit that profile.

The established mining companies are incredibly knowledgeable about geology and are skilled with dynamite and exotic heavy equipment; however, when winery owners are considering an investment of a couple hundred thousand dollars or undertaking a multimillion-dollar project, they often like the peace of mind that comes with a second opinion. Scott Lewis, an engineering geologist and tunneling consultant for Condor Earth Technologies, is the man to whom more than 150 wine-cave ventures have turned.

If you ask Scott about the geology of the area, he patiently explains many things, including how nice it is to encounter Sonoma welded tuff—a very consistent volcanic ash that has a psi of about 5,000. Drillers define rock hardness by psi, or how many pounds of pressure per square inch are required to crush a piece of material. Sonoma welded tuff is so consistent and stable that it could be left without shotcrete except that since the mid-'90s the practice has not been allowed unless approved by someone of Scott's credentials. If the rock is serpentine or highly fractured, the digging is going to be hard and treacherous. If the land is comprised of mud or clay, you may want to reconsider the project altogether.

Finding the perfect spot is not easy. Two or more portal sites are required for safety and operational reasons, and the construction of the interiors can be complicated by the various floorplans. The size of a typical wine cave is 13 to 18 feet wide and 10 to 13 feet high. Constructed caves, however, range up to 85 feet in width and 50 feet in height. On most occasions, the New Austrian Tunneling Method, also known as the Sequential Excavation Method, is used to excavate and support wine caves. Sometimes, drill and blast is used in combination with SEM.

The tunnels are usually excavated using a roadheader or a milling head attachment to an excavator. Initially the advance is likely to be limited to two feet without immediate support. Once turned under, the advance may proceed at four feet, six feet or even longer lengths before support is needed; but sheared serpentine, deeply weathered lava, wet clayey soil or other unstable rock conditions may limit the unsupported advance to less than two feet.

That reinforcement comes in the form of steel and a mix of 4,000 psi shotcrete. A minimum two-inch thickness of wet shotcrete is applied around the exposed ground perimeter following each day's advance. As cave dimensions and ground conditions require, additional layers of shotcrete and welded wire fabric follow on subsequent days. In some cases, rock bolts are also installed. Where wider and taller halls are used, modeling is employed to assist with liner design.

Interior finishing of the caves is an integral part of the construction process. Waterproofing details are an important consideration inside the wine caves. Most contractors install prefabricated drainage strips at regular intervals between the native ground and the shotcrete liner to relieve hydrostatic pressure. Where excessive groundwater is present, membranes have been placed between successive layers of shotcrete. The wine-cave industry in northern California is at the forefront of waterproofing technology implementation.

After the cave complex has been completely excavated, waterproofed and initially supported, a two-inch thickness of final shotcrete is applied to the walls and arch. A finished cave may have four to eight inches or more of concrete lining its interior.

Alf Burtleson

Alf Burtleson's name has become synonymous with the words wine cave—only fitting for the person who has been at the center of this renaissance, guiding it since the beginning. His expertise has been sought in developing industry codes, regulations and fire standards. He has set high expectations and is universally respected and appreciated by his peers and people throughout the world who build caves.

As a youth growing up in the foothills east of San Francisco, Alf became so good at golf that he won the northern California high school golf championship. That led to a scholarship to Stanford University in 1954, where he played for the university's team all four years while earning a degree in civil engineering.

Upon graduating in 1958, he worked for a consulting engineering firm—DeLeau, Cather & Company, which is now part of Parsons—with offices in Chicago and San Francisco. In 1960 he was hired by Charles Harney Construction Co.—builder of Candlestick Park and Caldecott Tunnel—as a project engineer on San Francisco's southern freeway.

When Mr. Harney died suddenly in 1962, without any business plan for such a situation, the business shut down. Alf was asked to take the leadership role of finishing projects in progress. Once he accomplished that, he and his colleagues were out of work, so at age 26 he formed his own company with a crew of two men doing small utility projects.

By 1972 he had established himself as a very competent civil engineer, building freeways, water tunnels and PG&E tunnels; however, the Beringer project gave him firsthand experience of wine caves. For a man who appreciated and had some understanding of wine and who also had the ability to build tunnels, going into the earth to store wine was something very logical and doable.

At that time Moet & Hennessy had come into the valley and were preparing to establish Chandon on the hills just west of Yountville. Alf's knowledge of the subject of wine included Chandon's association with caves in France; he began figuring up the cost of digging a cave that would be comparable to or less than the expense of a stand-up building to warehouse wine.

In 1973 Alf met the project manager to discuss doing caves and to give them prices. The Chandon project went a different direction, with the construction of a large cut-and-cover project, but Alf was ready with the cost all figured out if someone did come asking.

Alf and his wife, Mary, a musician and artist, have studied caves throughout the world. They would often share their knowledge and enthusiasm with clients. In a conversation with Alf and Mary one quickly realizes what a team they have been. They often finish each other's sentences. Alf will explain, "The clients were generally couples," and Mary will add, "Yes, it is usually a family affair," and Alf will add, "So it was good for us to be a couple, too," and Mary then adds, "Sometimes people are very intimidated by this heavy construction issue, so I certainly tried to comfort them, tell them how it worked and why it worked and sometimes I would draw so they could visualize and think of sculpting within the earth."

For Alf it was always about treating the clients as he would want to be treated, building the safest, strongest, most artistic space possible, and perhaps most importantly saving valuable agricultural land in the process. That he certainly accomplished.

In 2003 he sold his company to Jim and Lois Curry, who continue building caves under the Alf Burtleson Construction name, but he remains a consultant to the company.

Dale Wondergem

The spinning, grinding orb at the end of the Dosco's boom became an extension of Dale Wondergem's hands. Dale first worked on a cave project in 1967 when he achieved his blasting license on a four-mile bypass tunnel project for the San Francisco water district. Six years later, during a construction project at Stanford Stadium, he met and joined up with Alf Burtleson—a link that spanned 30 years. When Alf leased the roadheader in 1981, a man was sent by the manufacturer, Dosco, to assist with set-up and to demonstrate its operation. The company man seemed to have some difficulty controlling the machine, so Dale volunteered to give it a try.

From that time on Dale took charge of the mining equipment and became the roadheader operator. "Early on, my wife said I must have been building caves in my sleep, since I would move my hands back and forth as if controlling the levers." When he retired 25 years later, he had mined more than 40 wine caves—miles and miles of underground wine space. During those years he imparted his mining skills to his son Ricky, and they worked together on many projects. While leaving a legacy in the wine-cave story, Dale spent his spare time building and racing sprint cars.

There isn't much about going into the earth that he has not encountered. When Dale walks on a job, the confidence level is elevated; his opinions are honored by owners and engineers alike. He is recognized by everyone in the industry as the master of the roadheader, a sculptor of underground spaces. To the owners of those caves, Dale Wondergem is the hero who arrived at the site with a smile each morning and made it all happen.

Above: The 360-cubic-inch wing sprint car is one of Dale's many creations.

Facing Page Right: Dale and his son Ricky at the Château Boswell Winery cave.

Hawks & Hawks Wine Caves

Ever since they were kids Stephen and Edward Hawks have been digging in the Napa Valley dirt. "The human core has a real affinity for underground structure," says Stephen. "Deep inside us, we must all be cavemen at heart." The foundation they acquired while working in construction paved their way into the world of wine caves. In their case, form would certainly follow function. The sense of exploration into the earth has become very fascinating.

Experience is everything, which is why firsthand knowledge from their father Lyman Hawks and wine-cave guru Dale Wondergem has

meant so much to the Hawks brothers. Napa Valley is composed of volcanic soil. Every day you face something new; the type of ground changes every foot. This is part of the excitement, but you have to pay attention. "If you don't respect the ground," says Stephen, "Mother Earth will teach you a lesson." During one wine-cave dig, the Hawks & Hawks crew ran into a two-story ball of clay with the consistency of Jell-O. There was no way to go but forward!

Hawks & Hawks, a family-run company, dug its first wine cave in 2001 for Frazier Winery in Napa.

Glen Ragsdale—Underground Associates, Inc.

"It has been both a pleasure and an honor to develop relationships with our clients as we bring together their visions and our experience to create unique wine caves," says Glen Ragsdale, founder of Underground Associates. With each dig, the nuances of the project soon become apparent. The geology may offer interesting surprises, and the owners bring their own touches, turning sections of the wine cave into personal monuments—some have dining rooms underground, others have car museums.

As a child Glen moved from town to town with his family, as his father worked on major highway, dam and other construction projects. Early on, Glen's father mentored him in the ways of heavy equipment. After military service in the 101st Airborne Division, Glen worked his way up the tunneling side of construction, mastering the use of all types of tunneling equipment.

In 1978 Glen teamed with a childhood friend, Russell Clough, and developed Russell Clough/Underground Associates, concentrating on providing construction management for large tunneling contractors. In 1987 they brought their company to Napa Valley and

built their first wine cave at Pine Ridge Vineyards. In 1994 Russell was approached to teach at Stanford University, his alma mater, because his engineering background and years of experience would be ideal for teaching and inspiring engineering students. Russell is now a consulting professor of engineering at Stanford. He and his students visit the wine caves in Napa Valley as a part of their curriculum. Glen then joined with Graham Wozencroft, a very dedicated, talented and inspired engineer from England. Together they have created many significant wine caves.

The process of creating caves is utilitarian as well as an art form, since many caves are an expression of their owners. Each one is exciting: "The beginning and ending are the great moments of the wine-cave experience." After more than two decades of excavation, Glen still finds himself learning through each project.

Glen's 1978 Cessna T-210-M is a complex, high-performance, retractable-gear airplane with a true airspeed of 180 nautical miles per hour. Glen's wife, Shirley Ragsdale, designed the memorable paint job when the plane was completely refurbished in 2007 and outfitted with the best avionics package available.

Graham Wozencroft

When Graham Wozencroft emerged from the darkness into the sunlight at the completion of Stag's Leap Wine Cellars' cave, Warren Winiarski placed a wreath on his head. When the Palmaz Vineyards project came to an end the Palmaz family didn't want him to leave.

Graham Wozencroft is the brilliant superintendent and tunnel engineer for Underground Associates. Raised just outside of Ludlow, England, a stone's throw from the Welsh border, Graham has a lifelong passion for sports and cars. In 1973 he graduated from the University of Nottingham with honors and distinction and a degree in mining engineering.

His first practical experience was as an assistant safety officer in charge of four canaries. He would carry them in a cage on his visits to sites for gas detection through 20 miles of underground tunnels. Graham shares, "They are much more reliable than gas meters—when a canary stops singing and falls off the perch dead, it's time to get out!"

Immigrating to America in 1976 with the intention of learning more about shotcreting techniques, he experienced a good dose of cultural shock on his first job in the coalfields of West Virginia. His accounts of those days—including one when a miner's wife came down to the bottom of the mine and fired off a round from her 357 magnum—are a bit like reading a Hunter S. Thompson novel.

In 1979 he began working as a tunnel engineer with Russell Clough and Glen Ragsdale on a wastewater project in San Francisco. The chemistry between these guys was great, and over the course of the next seven years they worked together on projects in subzero weather in the mountains of Utah and rattlesnake-infested areas of California's central hills.

When Russell and Glen began creating wine caves in 1987, Graham joined them right after the first phase of the Pine Ridge job and for the next three years worked in all activities as a tunnel engineer and coordinator of the shotcrete—dry and wet mix—support systems.

In 1991 he left the area to focus on projects in San Francisco and Hawaii as a concrete engineer, pile-driving engineer and project manager. In 1994 he was project manager for an onshore/offshore

microtunnel under the ocean that received the International Microtunnel of the Year award. "Unfortunately, we had a hardhat diver fatality after the first of four drives. I was devastated and my heart was no longer in the project. Glen had finished the Archery Summit cave in Oregon and had picked up more work in Napa, so I decided to come back to Napa and dig wine caves."

Since coming back to Napa, he has helped shape over 350,000 square feet of wine caves. And after almost 40 years working every day in the tunneling business, he is a guy who has a lot of fun at work and whose enthusiasm for tunnel work is infectious.

Alf Burtleson Construction

Like any great flagship, Alf Burtleson Construction developed its name as the leader in the construction of wine caves, with more than three decades of expertise in subterranean problem solving, decisiveness and attention to detail.

When Alf retired in 2003, he sold the company to Jim and Lois Curry. Jim is an industry veteran with more than 30 years of experience building tunnels in the New York and Atlanta subway systems. Alf maintains a role in the company as a consultant and close advisor.

"We'll take on anything," says Jim. This is the legacy he picked up. Diligence, matched with a fair amount of risk-taking. "We construct tunnels, but at the end of the day, we turn them into wine caves," says Jim, and "each is unique with its own special, intimate ambience."

The Cave Company

After graduating from Stanford in 1995 with a master's degree in civil engineering, Vincent Georges gained practical experience working on and managing wine-cave projects. From laborer to roadheader operator and on to project manager, Vincent learned the trade from the ground up.

In 2006 he launched his own business, The Cave Company, where he demonstrates a daily dedication to safety, quality and teamwork. "It is my personal mission to be involved on a daily basis with each project that we undertake. Ultimately, our clients' satisfaction hinges on meeting their needs and expectations. I feel that this can be accomplished successfully through clear communication and attention to detail. Our goal is to be proud of every project we complete."

Beyond the practical uses and benefits, Vincent also sees the cave as a place of security and romance: "I enjoy giving cave tours—there always seems to be an air of mystery surrounding what might be hidden behind cave portal doors. When we are in the process of excavating new ground, there is a wonderful sense of discovery, of being where no one else has ever been. I feel lucky to be able to contribute to the romance that is a well-crafted wine." Vincent's passion for caves is contagious.

Top Left: Vincent Georges.

Middle Left: Wine cave in Oakville.

Bottom Left: Dutch Henry Winery cave.

Facing Page: O'Shaughnessy wine library.

Nordby Wine Caves

Just imagine how the hillsides and valley floors of Napa would look with a couple hundred more surface buildings. Nordby Wine Caves has actively worked to preserve the landscape as well as create underground solutions for wine-production needs. This is low-impact building with high rewards. The exceptional combination of an experienced crew, strong community partnerships, state-of-the-art equipment and an impressive portfolio has earned Nordby a solid reputation for underground construction.

President Rick Shone took the controls of Nordby Wine Caves in 2008 and continues to build on the success of Del and Craig Nordby's 1996 venture, Nordby Construction. Rick and Craig are partners in this thriving business. By offering a turnkey system of construction, Nordby Wine Caves develops underground spaces that allow not only optimal winery processes, but also remarkable caves that extend each winery's brand.

Magorian Mine Services

Alf Burtleson invited Don Magorian to assist with blasting during the construction of the Miner Family Vineyards wine cave in 1997. He saw in Don the skills and mindset required to create quality underground structures and encouraged Don to consider building wine caves in the valley.

Don was raised in a family that owned and operated underground mines and had a drilling business. With a background of mining and maintenance, he obtained a degree in mining engineering at the University of Nevada, Reno and became an underground mining and tunneling contractor soon afterward. Well versed at modifying equipment for specific needs, he started excavating wine caves and immediately deviated from the norm, modifying equipment for increased excavation efficiency and to better deal with difficult geology.

His perfectionist mentality shows in all of his projects. "My goal is not to follow the standards established by others, but to establish standards for others to follow," says Don.

"Challenges are always there," he continues. "The geology's different, owners have different desires and needs—it's just an opportunity to apply my architectural and engineering background." For Don, the reality is that no two projects are the same. "Our work is certainly not standard," he says. By optimizing equipment to better handle very difficult ground, always pushing the boundaries of efficiency and design, Magorian Mine Services produces projects with elements nobody's ever done before. Ensuring uniqueness, to Don, "makes for an eye-opening experience."

Lail Design Group, Inc.
Architecture & Planning

Jon Lail has long believed in the value of subterranean wine storage, which he had initially experienced in the 19th-century caves of his father-in-law's Inglenook Winery. His first opportunity to apply his wine knowledge to the design of a contemporary cave came with the development of Clos Pegase in 1985. Those caves soon became recognized as the model for a wine cave with "something more." Since that time, Jon and his team of architects and designers at Lail Design Group have embraced underground construction as an important component in their approach to environmentally responsible hillside winery design.

John believes that caves are "the most environmentally responsible way to store wine both in barrel and in bottle. Exterior aboveground structures require additional air conditioning, maintenance and a myriad of other expensive components." He even projects the future of the industry: "Caves may well become the most energy-efficient spaces available for human habitation. With the warming of the planet and other environmental changes, underground living could be in our future."

Lail Design Group understands that wine caves in Napa Valley are very personal, and every new client and site demands a unique response. While a cave's value for barrel storage is primary, it does not take long for one to recognize the fact that caves carry a romantic appeal, which elevates their value well above the utilitarian. There is a continuing desire to transform them into spaces that enhance the complete experience of wine. Today, Lail Design Group continues to successfully apply its creativity and attention to detail to the benefit of winery visitors, winemakers and, naturally, the wine.

Index

Acknowledgments

More than a decade ago, Alf Burtleson took a phone call from an inquisitive stranger and kindly invited me to see a cave being built. In the ensuing years, Alf has been most gracious. Dale Wondergem always had the time to share details and stories any time I called. Scott Lewis, Don Magorian, Graham Wozencroft, Glen Ragsdale, Stephen Hawks and Jim and Luke Curry have all been generous with their time.

I sincerely appreciate the warmth and hospitality of the many winery owners who have shared their personal thoughts and allowed me to photograph their caves.

My thanks to the team at Panache who did all the things they do so well to make the book a grand reality—Brian Carabet for his belief in the book, Rosalie Wilson and Daniel Reid for their attention to the words, Emily Kattan for her delightful disposition and design, and Kathryn Newell for her friendship and persistence in the field. And, of course, all the hidden faces and names behind the scenes.

My family has been patient and supportive. I wish my dad, Tulio, were still alive, as he put that first Nikon D1X in my hands in 2001 to make it so much easier. And Mum, thank you for always being there for me—we saw it through. I owe large thanks also to my brother-in-law, Nick, and the dogs Flap and Whoozie for giving up their Jeanne so often this last year to stay out with Mum. I couldn't have done it without you, Jeanne.

Nor could I without Donn and Molly Chappellet who opened their home and hearts to me as family. Molly's attention and contribution to the design of this book has been so important. Her continual support and encouragement as a mentor, collaborator and friend is immeasurable.

Daniel D'Agostini

Thank you, Daniel, for your stick-to-it-tive-ness: your always gentle response, your patience and, above all, your stunning photographs. You have made this project a joy! I'm glad I stopped carrying my camera after the first few caves; there was no need.

I add my thanks to friends in the Valley, old and new, who entered into this project with us, allowing us to photograph their magnificent sanctuaries.

Panache has been a dream publisher: Brian, who could solve any problem, Kitty, with her invaluable perseverance, Emily, for her ability to create and recreate so agreeably, and Rosalie for filling in the gaps.

Thank you to Jayne Unander and Luanne Wells, my two sisters: Jayne, for her constant encouragement and editorial assistance; Luanne, for challenging and pushing me to do better. Each has been so important in my life and in my journey into the book world.

And to my husband, Donn, and his early vision and desire to make exceptional wines, which brought us to Napa Valley 42 years ago.

Molly Chappellet

Published by

PANACHE PARTNERS

Panache Partners, LLC
1424 Gables Court
Plano, Texas 75075
469.246.6060
Fax: 469.246.6062
www.panache.com

Publishers: Brian G. Carabet and John A. Shand
Regional Publisher: Kathryn Newell
Senior Graphic Designer: Emily A. Kattan
Editors: Daniel Reid and Rosalie Wilson
Managing Production Coordinator: Kristy Randall

Written by Daniel D'Agostini with Molly Chappellet

Page 1: Ironstone Vineyards
Pages 2-3: Antica Napa Valley
Page 6: Forman Vineyard
Page 234: Roadheader at Porter Family Vineyards
Pages 236-237: Vineyard just north of St. Helena
Page 239: Long Meadow Ranch

Contributing Photographers:
Sam Aslanian, page 194 bottom
Marla Bleecher, page 174 top and middle
Susan Boswell, page 219 right
William Brouwer, page 71
Marc Boldin, page 170 bottom, 171
Cordero Studio, page 39 top
Bill Fuchs, page 231 bottom
Adrian Gregorutti, page 40 top
Thomas Percival, page 206
Erhard Pfeiffer, pages 112-113 top
Cesar Rubio, page 207 top
Chuck Stefanetti, pages 52-53

Printed in Malaysia

Distributed by Independent Publishers Group
800.8884741

PUBLISHER'S DATA

Into the Earth: A Wine Cave Renaissance

Library of Congress Control Number: 2009930015
ISBN 13: 978-1-933415-82-6
ISBN 10: 1-933415-82-7

First Printing 2009
10 9 8 7 6 5 4 3 2 1

Panache Partners, LLC is dedicated to the restoration and conservation of the environment. Our books are
manufactured with strict adherence to an environmental management system in accordance with ISO 14001
standards, including the use of paper from mills certified to derive their products from environmentally
managed forests. We are committed to continued investigation of alternative paper products and
environmentally responsible manufacturing processes to ensure the preservation of our fragile planet.

For information about custom editions, special sales, or premium and corporate books, please contact
Panache Partners at bcarabet@panache.com